PROFILES IN BLACK AND WHITE

STORIES OF MEN AND WOMEN WHO FOUGHT AGAINST SLAVERY

Illustration by Jennifer Perrott

PROFILES IN BLACK AND WHITE

STORIES OF MEN AND WOMEN WHO FOUGHT AGAINST SLAVERY

ILLUSTRATED WITH PHOTOGRAPHS AND ENGRAVINGS

1366

BY ELIZABETH F. CHITTENDEN

CHARLES SCRIBNER'S SONS   NEW YORK

To F. S. U. and the C. K.'s with gratitude

An adaptation of "Alien
Daughters" was first
published in *Yankee* magazine.

Copyright © 1973 Elizabeth F. Chittenden

1 3 5 7 9 11 13 15 17 19 C/C 20 18 16 14 12 10 8 6 4 2

Printed in the United States of America
Library of Congress Catalog Card Number 73–2929
SBN 684–13387–3 (cloth)

CONTENTS

v

LIST OF ILLUSTRATIONS

ACKNOWLEDGMENTS

To the many librarians and the curators of historical societies and museums who have given their time and who have helped me find materials, I wish to express my thanks:

Ernest Kaiser of The Schomburg Center for Research in Black Culture, The New York Public Library; Claude E. Moore, Jr. of the Association for the Study of Negro Life and History, Washington, D. C.; Caroline Spicer, reference librarian of the Cornell University Library, Ithaca, New York; Jerry Kearns, head of the Reference Section of the Library of Congress; Mrs. Granville T. Prior, director of the South Carolina Historical Society, Charleston, South Carolina; June N. Lollis, registrar of the Gibbes Art Gallery, Charleston, South Carolina; Margaret Nelson of the Essex Institute, Salem, Massachusetts; Ernest S. Dodge of the Peabody Museum, Salem, Massachusetts; Dr. Dorothy Parker, librarian of the Moorland-Singarn Collection of Howard University, Washington, D. C.; Jack Jackson of the Art Department of The Boston Athenaeum; and William Loos of the Rare Books Department of the Buffalo-Erie County Library.

My gratitude also goes to friends who have helped with photography: Dorothy Ralph, Charles Goodrich, and Mary Bohne.

To Anne Diven, the editor with whom I have been fortunate enough to work, I want to express my deep appreciation and thanks.

E.F.C.

AUTHOR'S INTRODUCTION

The past with its good and its evil lives in the present. What men and women did a hundred years ago has shaped our world today. And we in turn, by our actions today, will shape tomorrow's world.

Most of us are familiar with the leaders of the abolitionist movement in America. Many books have been written about Frederick Douglass, Harriet Beecher Stowe, Sojourner Truth, John Brown, Harriet Tubman, and William Lloyd Garrison. But for any crusade to succeed, it must have in its ranks thousands of dedicated people. These self-sacrificing daring men and women give of themselves, work without tiring, carry out mundane directions, and even risk their lives for their beliefs. Often their names are forgotten.

For the most part these are the men and women whose stories are told in *Profiles in Black and White*. Whenever possible original dialogue has been used in these stories of blacks and whites who worked together and alone to achieve the noblest of human concepts—freedom of the body and freedom of the spirit for every individual.

1

LIKE OTHER BOSTON BOYS

WILLIAM NELL

"Quiet!" the principal demanded. "We have a distinguished visitor. Mr. Lovell has been so kind as to come to tell us the results of last week's examinations."

For the past week, as he tramped the long walk to Smith School, one of Boston's schools for black children, William Nell had dreamed of this moment. He had always won highest honors in Smith School. But this year he and a few other blacks had been allowed to take the intermediate examinations given to pupils in Boston's white schools. William was eager to know if he could win honors in competition with white boys and girls. If so, he would receive a beautiful silver Franklin Medal.

This December morning in 1829, the white principal of Smith School had called all the intermediate

3

grades to the shabby assembly hall. The white examiner, Mr. Lovell, sat beside the principal on the platform. There weren't enough seats for all the pupils, and some stood along the wall at the side.

Slight in body, serious in manner and expression for his thirteen years, William Nell sat with his eyes glued on Mr. Lovell, who was talking now: ". . . the splendid Smith School, which gives so much to you young people, which is run just for you boys and girls. . . . and three pupils, three of your friends, have brought glory to your school by passing the examinations with honor. I am pleased to announce the names: William Cooper Nell and. . . ." The voice droned on.

Stunned with excitement and relief, William heard only his own name. He couldn't believe it. The boy next to him poked him and whispered, "Hey, there, you're to go up to the front. Didn't you hear?"

William felt his blood rise up, flooding his cheeks, as he walked to the platform. He had won the handsome Franklin Medal!

Standing in line with the other two winners, William straightened his shoulders and listened to Mr. Lovell. "I am pleased to present to each of you a book about an American whom you will do well to emulate. As token of your extraordinary success in your examinations, I give you a biography of Benjamin Franklin."

But the Medal? William knew every winner was

4

supposed to get a Franklin Medal, not a book. He waited for the Medal. Mr. Lovell handed them the books and shook their hands. That was all. With reluctance, William accepted his award. He was not like other Boston boys after all.

His parents were proud of their son.

"Look," his mother boasted to her husband that afternoon when he returned from his tailor shop. "See what our William was given today for doing so well in the examinations." She smoothed the book's cover with her hand before giving it to his father.

William snatched it from his father and ran into his room. They just didn't understand that the book was an insult, not an honor. He swung the closet door open and flung the book in the corner.

"Your name's in the paper." His father came into the room with the evening newspaper in his hand. "See, son, here's your name. And it says, 'Mayor Otis is having a dinner for all the . . .'" His father stopped reading aloud.

"Let me see." William felt anger and hurt as he read the rest of the article to himself: ". . . a dinner for all the white winners of the Franklin Medals at Faneuil Hall next Wednesday evening."

Even at thirteen, William was determined to do something about this discrimination. He began making inquiries and found a friend who often waited on table at banquets. He was to serve at the Franklin dinner.

"I've just as much right there as those white boys! And I'm going! Let me wait on table for you part of the time," William urged and his friend finally agreed to William's scheme.

The evening of the dinner, William, dressed in a waiter's jacket, brought in a tray. He looked over the faces of the winners. With aplomb, he set the mayor's plate before him, then another plate before the examiner, Mr. Lovell.

Mr. Lovell recognized him. "You ought to be here with the other boys," he whispered.

William stared back angrily at the examiner, and the white man dropped his eyes in embarrassment. The boy could say nothing, but inwardly he thought, "That's what you say! Why, then, didn't you see that I was asked?"

William Nell never forgot the pain and anguish of those moments. Much later he said of the incident, "The impression created on my mind by this day's experience deepened into a solemn vow, 'God helping me, I will do my best to hasten the day when the color of the skin is no barrier to truly equal school rights.' "

The Nells, like the bulk of Boston's Negro community, lived on the back side of Beacon Hill—the side Boston called "nigger hill." To go to the only

6

intermediate school for Negroes, William and all the other black children had to walk past five white schools which they were not allowed to enter. There was no high school for blacks. If any, like William Nell, wanted an education beyond the intermediate level, a kind teacher might try to provide some more advanced instruction.

After his graduation from Smith School, Nell worked in the law office of W. Bowditch, a prominent white abolitionist, and thought of becoming a lawyer himself. He also became active in the abolitionist cause, led by such men as William Lloyd Garrison and Wendell Phillips. Abolitionists believed in the abolishment of slavery. Phillips persuaded Nell not to enter law. To become a member of the bar, Phillips reasoned, a man had to take an oath to support the United States Constitution, which gave white men the right to own, sell, and retrieve slaves. Certainly no sincere abolitionist, especially a black man, could swear loyalty to any proslavery document.

Instead of becoming a lawyer, William Nell involved himself in various other fields. As a business agent, he prepared deeds and mortgages; he worked as an accountant and a bill collector; and he ran an employment agency for Negroes. For Garrison's journal, *The Liberator*, he wrote articles against segregation and about black activities in Boston. He even went to Rochester, New York, for a time to help

7

Wendell Phillips, a friend and fellow abolitionist, who persuaded William Nell not to enter law. Library of Congress

Frederick Douglass, the black abolitionist and former slave, with his famous paper, *North Star.* Later in his life, Nell was appointed a postal clerk, the first Negro to hold a position under the federal government.

The poet John Greenleaf Whittier gave Nell the idea of writing about the contributions of blacks to the American Revolution. Whittier, a Quaker, believed firmly in nonviolence and was against "eulogizing the shedding of blood." Yet he told Nell that if white revolutionary war heroes were to be honored, black heroes should also be honored. Nell's own father had been a steward on a ship which escaped from the British blockade in the War of 1812.

As a result, Nell collected detailed and accurate information on black men like Crispus Attucks, the very first man to die in the Revolution. In 1852 Nell's book *Services of Colored Americans in the Wars of 1776 and 1812* was published; and in 1855 a revised

8

edition, *Colored Patriots of the American Revolution*, came out. Whittier had a statement in the preface of each volume, and Harriet Beecher Stowe, an author and abolitionist, wrote the introduction to the second.

While studying early black history in America, Nell was also making new black history. He went to all-black political conventions throughout New York State. More and more, as he participated in these segregated meetings, he came to oppose all kinds of segregation. He advocated integration in the churches. Because he felt it would be more effective, he urged Negroes to work against slavery within white abolitionist groups. He said, "Negroes should abandon separate action and become part and parcel of the general community."

The ideal target for such integration was the Boston public schools, the only ones in the state still segregated in 1846, although Massachusetts had abolished slavery by judicial decision in 1783.

Around 1800, Boston Negroes had sought separate black schools because they feared that their sons and daughters could not meet white competition or withstand harassment by resentful white schoolchildren. By the 1840s, however, their mood had changed, and they were willing to fight to abolish these segregated schools.

In 1840, William Nell and a group of Negro and white abolitionists began a campaign to wipe out

COLORED PATRIOTS

OF THE

AMERICAN REVOLUTION,

WITH SKETCHES OF SEVERAL

DISTINGUISHED COLORED PERSONS:

TO WHICH IS ADDED A BRIEF SURVEY OF THE

Condition and Prospects of Colored Americans.

By WM. C. NELL.

WITH AN INTRODUCTION BY

HARRIET BEECHER STOWE.

BOSTON:

PUBLISHED BY ROBERT F. WALLCUT.

1855.

A reproduction of the title page from the revised edition of William Nell's book, Colored Patriots of the American Revolution. *Rare Books Department, Buffalo-Erie County Library* segregation from the Boston schools. For eleven long years they fought doggedly to achieve this goal.

Nell is chiefly remembered for this accomplishment, which was the fulfillment of his boyhood vow to effect true equality and educational opportunity for all children regardless of color.

Their first target was the Smith School. Housing all grades, it was woefully inadequate: primary grades on the first floor, intermediate grades and a limited amount of advanced work on the second. The building, the equipment, and the training of the teachers were inferior to those in the white public schools. In addition, Abner Forbes, the white principal, did not take the time to understand the black pupils and their problems. He often gave cruel and unfair punishment.

"Mr. Forbes thinks my boy and girl aren't bright. He thinks no black boy or girl is bright. He shouldn't teach black children," Negro parents complained.

On Nell's advice, they took their complaints to the

An old engraving of black children being denied entrance to a school for whites. The Schomburg Collection, New York City

Boston School Committee, which after investigation declared Principal Forbes blameless, but advised his transfer. He remained, however, for the rest of the school year.

Nell began a barrage of petitions to the School Committee. With a long list of distinguished signatures, his first petition asked for further investigation of the separate schools. A group appointed by the School Committee upheld segregation: "The continuance of the separate schools for colored children is not only legal and just, but is adapted to promote the education of that part of our population." The report went on to accuse black children of irregular attendance. They would hurt the standard of work of white children, the committee maintained. "The difference between the black and white races lies deep in the physical, mental, and moral natures of the two races. No integration will erase these differences."

Nell's corps of protesters not only continued their volley of petitions but set up test cases.

Little Sarah Roberts was only six years old. The walk to Smith School from her home was a long one. One cold February morning in 1847, her father walked with her to the nearest neighborhood school, which was for white children.

Outside the door, he gave her a slip of paper demanding her admittance to the first grade. "Give this to the teacher. She will find you a place in her class."

But when the teacher saw the black girl entering her class of white boys and girls, she said, "What are you doing here? You have made a mistake. This isn't the school you belong in!" The voice was harsh and frightening to Sarah.

The child said nothing and handed the teacher the paper her father had given her. The teacher took it, glanced at it, and tore it up. "This paper doesn't give you the right to be here. Get out of this building at once and go to the school where you belong."

As Sarah turned away from the woman towering over her, she caught a glimpse of the sea of white faces staring at her. She fixed her eyes on the door and walked to it. She fumbled through her tears for the handle, turned it, and stepped outside.

Once outside, she ran—raced—to her father, who had told her he would wait awhile at the front of the building in case she should need him. He caught her up in his arms.

"I'm here, Sarah. They didn't hurt you, did they?" Under his breath, he said, "They'll pay for what they've done to her!"

Later that same year, Sarah's father, Benjamin Roberts, brought suit against the city of Boston for violating the Massachusetts statute which declared that any child unlawfully excluded from public school instruction could recover damage from the city or town excluding him. The case went to the Massachusetts Supreme Court with Charles Sumner acting as

13

counsel for the plaintiff, Benjamin Roberts. Sumner, a distinguished statesman who later became a senator from Massachusetts, was an early advocate of freeing the slaves.

Sumner argued that according to the Massachusetts Bill of Rights "all men are born equal," and all children, regardless of color or race, are entitled to the benefits of our public schools. The state supreme court was impressed but ruled in favor of the Boston School Committee. The ruling, supporting Jim Crow, or segregated schools, implied that equality and segregation could legally exist side by side.

Nell attacked next by proposing a tax boycott. If blacks moved to nearby towns where the schools were already integrated, they would not only solve their children's educational problems but hurt the city financially. In *The Liberator* Nell wrote, "Boston's fast losing many of her intelligent, worthy, aspiring citizens, who are becoming taxpayers in adjoining localities, for the sole advantage of equal rights."

John Hilton, a barber prominent in the fight, moved to Cambridge, where his daughter, who had been doing poorly in Smith School, took honors with her white classmates.

Before school opened in September, 1849, Nell called a meeting of Negro parents and other interested blacks in the Belknap Street Baptist Church. To overcome school segregation, he suggested a school boycott.

ARGUMENT

OF

CHARLES SUMNER, ESQ.

AGAINST THE

CONSTITUTIONALITY OF SEPARATE COLORED SCHOOLS,

IN THE CASE OF

SARAH C. ROBERTS *vs.* THE CITY OF BOSTON.

———

Before the Supreme Court of Mass., Dec 4, 1849.

〰〰〰〰〰〰〰

BOSTON:
PUBLISHED BY B. F. ROBERTS,
1849.

PRINTED AT NO. 3 CORNHILL.

Title page from Charles Sumner's brief for the Sarah C. Roberts case. The Schomburg Collection, New York City

"Take your young people out of this separate school. Do all you can without violence—I repeat, without violence—to keep all children from entering Smith School." As he spoke, stones broke two of the church windows, hitting one man. "We will surround the school but use no trophies like these." Nell picked up one of the stones. "We resort to no such methods of appeal!"

The day the school opened, boycotters were at the school early. The crowd was orderly, although opponents described them as "a collection of rude boys, . . . all of them persons of color who beset the doors in a disorderly manner."

The school opened, but only twenty-three children registered. The Boston School Committee responded by appointing a well-qualified Negro, a Dartmouth man, as principal of Smith School. Nell fought back with more petitions. Attendance steadily dropped at Smith School. Through *The Liberator* Nell kept the cause before black and white sympathizers. These people gave sufficient money to open temporary schools so that no child would suffer. Because of these independent schools and the exodus of blacks to the suburbs of Boston, attendance continued to drop.

Under Nell's leadership, integrationists began an intensified campaign of petitioning. *The Liberator* published a suggested form for petitions. In 1855, with 1,500 signatures, Nell was at last victorious. Both houses of the state legislature passed a law forbidding discrimination because of color or religion in the public school system.

Next Nell resolved that integration, once achieved, must go smoothly. He took black parents to meet their children's new teachers. He met with parents and reminded them of their responsibilities.

On the first day of school integration, the windows on the front side of Beacon Hill were filled with curious faces watching black children on their way to neighborhood schools. To Nell's relief, only two children chose to go to Smith School, and soon the city closed it for lack of attendance.

The schools opened with little or no trouble. The Boston *Evening Telegraph* commented: "The introduction of the colored youth into the schools, we are happy to say, was accomplished with general good feeling on the part of both teachers and white children!"

That morning, September 3, 1855, just before time for school to open, William Nell stood in front of Smith School. A black boy, not far from him, was staring at the building. Suddenly the youth shook his fists at the school and shouted, "Good-bye forever, colored school! Today we're like other Boston boys!"

"God willing, like other Boston boys," Nell thought to himself, as he recalled a thirteen-year-old boy who had been given a book instead of a prized medal and a seat at a banquet table.

An early portrait of Prudence Crandall by Francis Alexander.
Cornell University

IN CANTERBURY TOWN

PRUDENCE CRANDALL

"You read and write, Sarah?" Prudence Crandall, headmistress of the Canterbury Academy for Young Ladies, asked the young Negro girl.

Sarah was waiting for her sister, Marcia, the hired girl, to finish clearing up after supper.

"Oh, yes, Ma'am, a little. I went to District School. But I want to get more learning—if I could, enough to teach other Negro children someday."

Why shouldn't Sarah learn enough to teach? The question rang in Prudence Crandall's mind. Her Quaker background had made her long see slavery as a sin. She had read some copies of the abolitionist journal *The Liberator*, which Marcia had borrowed from her fiancé. It had increased Miss Crandall's desire to help abolish slavery.

19

About a year earlier, in 1831, Prudence Crandall, a woman of twenty-nine, had opened an exclusive school for young ladies in Canterbury, Connecticut. Using all her capital and even going somewhat into debt, she bought the large white house with its classical pilasters at the southwest corner of the village green.

The school was proving successful with some twenty-six girls from leading families of Canterbury and neighboring towns. The townspeople felt the new school was indeed an asset to their community.

Now, as Prudence looked at Sarah Harris, a girl in her early teens, she thought: Here is a school, and here is a girl who wants to learn. And education is the best way to help Negroes abolish slavery. She knew that was why slave owners feared any learning for their black men and women, feared it so deeply that they made it a crime to teach slaves. But Sarah was a free Negro in a free state, for Connecticut as early as 1784 had passed an act which required the gradual freeing of all slaves living within its borders. Why shouldn't she have the opportunity to learn to teach free black children? Sarah *is* going to learn!

"Would you like to enter my school, Sarah?"

"What, Ma'am? What'd you say?"

"I asked if you wanted to come to school here to learn."

"Yes, Ma'am, but . . ."

20

"Why not? You can sleep at home and come here every day for lessons. The first class begins at eight in the morning. Come Monday, Sarah."

Sarah and Marcia stared silently at Miss Crandall, as she started to leave the kitchen. The charged silence made her look back.

"Sarah, you *do* want to study?"

Sarah nodded, speechless. Just as the slender upright woman had nearly closed the door, Sarah burst out, "But, Ma'am, I don't have any—"

"Money." Prudence Crandall finished the sentence. "Of course not. I'll take care of that. Monday —oh, no, Sarah," she said with embarrassment as the girl caught her hand and kissed it. She withdrew the hand but gently patted the girl's head.

The same evening, Prudence spoke to the young ladies in her school. "There is a girl, Sarah Harris, whom some of you may have seen and talked with. She wants to teach Negro children. If you are willing, I have decided to admit her to our school."

The girls, almost unanimously, wanted to have her study in the academy.

Monday, Prudence Crandall led Sarah Harris to the white pupils, who were gathered for a short prayer and silent meditation before the work of the day.

Miss Crandall introduced her. "We have a new pupil whom you will welcome, I know."

The girls were cordial. As the week progressed, they forgot she was in any way different from them. Sarah also gained assurance. She was going to be a quick pupil in books, Prudence thought. Her eagerness to learn would soon put her ahead of the others if they were not careful. Prudence rejoiced even though several disturbing incidents had already taken place.

The first had occurred the previous Wednesday evening when the wife of the Episcopal clergyman called on Miss Crandall.

"I come as your friend, Miss Crandall, about a rumor I fear is true. I have heard that you have a new pupil, a colored girl, in the school. It is true?"

"It is." Prudence spoke in a low, unfaltering voice.

"Are you aware what this unseemly mingling of a Negro, however worthy she may be, with the young white ladies will mean?"

"What?"

"The whites will be withdrawn from your school."

"But the other girls like Sarah Harris. She is a promising young lady herself. She is no different from the others—only more eager to learn than they."

"Young lady indeed! Sarah Harris went through the district school, enough schooling for any nigger wench! And parents will not have it said their daughters are going to school with a nigger! Your school will have to close if you keep the girl."

"Let it sink then, for I shall not turn her out!"

"Remember, Miss Crandall, I have warned you." The visitor swept out of the house and flounced down the front steps.

The next day the grocery boy asked to speak with Miss Crandall.

"Tell him to put the order on the kitchen table as usual," she told Marcia, who had summoned her.

"But he hasn't any groceries, Miss."

"No groceries? But I ordered . . . I'd better see him myself."

"Well, Ned, where are the groceries I ordered?"

"Oh, Miss Crandall!" Ned's cheeks were burning. He couldn't find words.

"Speak up, boy!"

"Miss—Miss Crandall, Mr. Smith said he wouldn't."

"He wouldn't what, Ned?"

"He's not selling to you anymore!"

"Not selling to me! But I've bought groceries from him ever since I opened the school. He solicited my first order. What's his reason?"

"You got a black, he says, going to school with the white ladies. He's not selling to you!"

So that was it. Prudence stiffened her back and straightened the stiff organdy neckpiece over the shoulders of her gray dress. Her deep-set eyes flashed.

"Tell Mr. Smith I shall purchase my food elsewhere." She turned on her heel and left Ned gaping.

But Miss Crandall did not find it easy. There was another grocery store in town. "Sorry, Miss Crandall, I'd like to but . . ." the proprietor told her. Other kinds of stores, the dry goods and the apothecary shop, closed their doors to her.

Parents began withdrawing their daughters from the school. Soon Sarah Harris was the only pupil left. Marcia was the single helper now, not that more were needed.

Prudence Crandall consulted with her friend, the Reverend Samuel May. On his advice she decided to open a new school in April—one for young Negro women who wanted more education. Mr. William Lloyd Garrison agreed to recruit the young ladies for her. They would come from all over the northeastern part of the country.

This notice, announcing Prudence Crandall's intention to open a school for young black women, appeared in The Liberator, *February 25, 1833. The New York Public Library*

PRUDENCE CRANDALL,
Principal of the Canterbury, (Conn.) Female Boarding School,

RETURNS her most sincere thanks to those who have patronized her School, and would give information that on the first Monday of April next, her School will be opened for the reception of young Ladies and little Misses of color. The branches taught are as follows:—Reading, Writing, Arithmetic, English Grammar, Geography, History, Natural and Moral Philosophy, Chemistry, Astronomy, Drawing and Painting, Music on the Piano, together with the French language.

☞ The terms, including *board, washing,* and tuition, are $25 per quarter, one half paid in advance.

☞ Books and Stationary will be furnished on the most reasonable terms.

For information respecting the School, reference may be made to the following gentlemen, viz:—Arthur Tappan, Esq., Rev. Peter Williams, Rev. Theodore Raymond, Rev. Theodore Wright, Rev. Samuel C. Cornish, Rev. George Bourne, Rev. Mr. Hayborn, *New-York city;*—Mr. James Forten, Mr. Joseph Cassey, *Philadelphia, Pa.;*—Rev. S. J. May, *Brooklyn, Ct.;*—Rev. Mr. Beman, *Middletown, Ct.;*—Rev. S. S. Jocelyn, *New-Haven, Ct.;*—Wm. Lloyd Garrison, Arnold Buffum, *Boston, Mass.;*—George Benson, *Providence, R. I.* Canterbury, (Ct.) Feb. 25, 1833.

She made no secret of her decision. She told her father, who had been driving his horse and buggy to neighboring villages for her necessary supplies. A kindly Quaker, he approved her plan.

"I'm proud of you, daughter. But it will be hard, you understand."

The shocking news spread quickly.

The town of Canterbury in Windham County of eastern Connecticut prided itself on its public spirit and high character. It boasted a reading club and a temperance movement. And of course it had high regard for Negro people—in their place. But a school for Negro girls on the green and opposite the handsome house State Attorney Andrew T. Judson had built! Never in Canterbury!

So, on March 9, 1833, Canterbury citizens called a town meeting. The voices of selectmen and others exploded from the floor.

"Negro girls coming in hordes to New England! To Canterbury!"

"Open the door and New England will become a Liberia of America!"

"Think of our women. Black men might try to marry our girls." The whisper leapfrogged through the meeting.

"Your homes will be next to worthless," Attorney Judson prophesied.

"Doesn't Miss Crandall know the law?"

Prudence Crandall knew all too well the Connecticut Black Law passed by the legislature the year before in Hartford. It made the establishment of a school for Negroes from out of state illegal unless the town approved.

"And we won't have such a school here in Canterbury!"

"We'll teach Prudence Crandall to stay within the law!"

Prudence Crandall ignored the Black Law.

In April Negro young ladies made their pilgrimage to Canterbury to study with Miss Crandall. They came from Philadelphia, Boston, New York, and Providence.

She would meet the different girls at the stagecoach and walk with them across the green to the white colonial house with its white picket fence.

Hoodlums would dog their heels, insulting the black girls and the white schoolmistress.

"We'll teach 'em—more than reading and writing!"

Miss Crandall would ignore the boys and engage the girls in conversation.

For their exercise during the spring, Miss Crandall would walk along the Canterbury lanes with her black pupils. Snowdrops dotting lawns gave way to violets; golden dandelions blanketed a meadow; apple blossoms and purple lilacs scented the air. One afternoon a rock from a slingshot burst through a hedge of syringa. It bruised the arm of a young student named

Florence. She winced but otherwise disregarded the blow.

"Niggers, niggers, Miss Crandall's out with her niggers."

Trying to ignore the shouts, Miss Crandall conducted her girls back to the shelter of the school. "Savages, Canterbury savages!" she cried, once they were safely inside.

Just then, Sarah Harris, who had been on the way to the school from her home, burst into the hall. "They blasted a horn right into my ear," she sobbed. "I can't hear."

Miss Prudence, as the girls fondly called her, decided Dr. Harris must see both Florence and Sarah. After supper she walked down the green to the doctor's, went to the door, and sounded the knocker. Dr. Harris himself came to the door. A look of consternation spread across his face when he saw Prudence Crandall.

"Dr. Harris, two of my young ladies—" she began.

"Your Negroes sick?"

"Well, . . . attacked by townspeople. Will you come to take care of them?"

As if to justify himself, he worked himself into a nasty rage. "Who ever heard of genuine doctors for Negroes? Why don't you take them to the horse doctor? There's one in Black Hill. Good evening, Miss Crandall."

"But, Doctor—"

"Good evening, I said." He slammed the door in her face.

Incredulous, dazed, Prudence Crandall walked back to her school. There was no other doctor in the small town. And if there were, would he come? The Reverend Samuel May would have to find a doctor for her girls.

She stretched tall for her height as she opened the school door. She hardly had time to wipe the anger from her face and assume a smile before she faced the ring of anxious faces, all looking to her for reassurance. She had to go on!

First the stores and now the doctor refused to serve them! Even a church had barred its doors to these innocent girls, who wanted only to learn!

It had happened three Sundays ago. The students had gone together to the Congregational church. At the door a deacon had met them. "You know, Miss Crandall, no race mixing in this church!"

The Friends Meeting in Black Hill and the Baptist church in Packerville were willing to receive them. It was understood, of course, that they were to sit in the back pews or the gallery near the door.

They set out for church. But when the stagecoach that went through Black Hill stopped, the driver leaned down and shouted, "No room for niggers! Nor for nigger lovers either!"

After these experiences the Reverend May conducted a private service in the school for the pupils.

Now the young ladies took their daily exercise inside the picket fence. For the past week as they filed out to walk up and down the garden paths, a church bell tolled and pistols were fired into the air. Once a cannon was set off. Always a crowd lined the outside of the fence shouting insults and threats.

And there was the incident of another student, Ann Eliza Hammond, of Providence, Rhode Island. The town officers had chosen her as a test case and invoked the pauper and vagrant laws against her. Unless she left town or her maintenance was guaranteed, she was to be whipped on her naked body not exceeding ten lashes. Friends and abolitionists raised a $10,000 bond guaranteeing her maintenance.

After the episode, a pupil from Boston remarked, "How delightful are the house, the green, the elm-lined streets of Canterbury. All that is lacking is civilized men to complete the scene."

One morning before breakfast, Marcia called Miss Crandall with urgency in her voice. "See, see what they've done!"

She handed Miss Prudence a pitcher of water just taken from the well. The water was discolored and foul with pieces of manure which must have been thrown into the well during the night.

"And they've thrown eggs all over the front of the house," Marcia panted.

"Primitive creatures, boors!" Prudence said sadly.

The well, their only source of water, was befouled.

No neighbor would give them so much as a glass of water. Miss Crandall's father had to carry it in to them by the bucketful and at the risk of high fines for visiting his daughter!

On an August afternoon, Prudence saw two officers marching to her door. Her father, who was discussing the situation with her, accompanied her as she went to meet them.

"You are under arrest for violation of the state Black Law," an officer said.

"You make me ashamed of our state, our town, our color, Justice Adams. Arrest me; put me in prison!" she defied him.

"We will gladly accept bail."

"I have money. At what is it set?" her father asked as he put his hand into his pocket.

"No, Father. I wish to be arrested. Perhaps it will awaken the people."

Prudence Crandall walked to the town jail between the two officers. Disturbed townspeople followed close. They watched a reluctant keeper swing open the door of the one-celled building. With apprehension they saw Prudence Crandall step into the cell recently occupied by a murderer.

The Reverend May offered her help. "If you now hesitate, if you dread the gloomy place so much as to wish to be saved from it, I will give bonds for you even now."

"Oh, no. I was only afraid they would *not* put me in jail."

Feeling confident that her arrest and imprisonment were enough to focus attention on the injustice of the Black Law, Prudence Crandall accepted bail the next day.

In the two trials which followed, she was declared guilty, but in an appeal to the state Supreme Court she was finally acquitted.

The school was kept open all this time by her sisters and some friends. Once declared innocent, she returned to her post at the school.

A few nights after her return to Canterbury, she woke suddenly from a sound sleep. She sensed danger. She smelled smoke coming from below. Not waiting to slip on her robe, she snatched the pitcher from the washstand and dashed down the stairs. In her office a fire smoldered, and the smoke had gone up the chimney to her room above. She doused the smoldering flame and put out the fire. But who had set it?

On September 9, a week later, the house lay dark. The headmistress had turned down the wick of her lamp and blown out the flame. That evening she had been assessing her and the school's situation, especially the safety of the nineteen young ladies who were progressing so rapidly in reading, writing, mathematics, and, most important, coming to a greater realization of their responsibility to others of their race. Nothing must harm her girls.

At her window, in the darkness, she sat for a moment in contemplation. The village clock struck twelve.

Suddenly she grew taut. Below she heard whispers, then shouts, stamping feet, and shattering glass. Clubs beat against the door and windows. A rock crashed through a window below and thudded against something. Now through her window she could see a mob of men with iron bars and flaming torches. She leaped back from the window as a rock spun past her and shattered the glass candlestick on her bedside table.

A recent photograph of Prudence Crandall's house in Canterbury. The Associated Publishers, Inc.

She rushed to the front room across the hall. "Girls, go to the back bedrooms. Barbarians are tossing rocks at women." She sounded defiant and brave, but for the first time she quailed within for the safety of her girls.

Once they were out of immediate danger, she felt renewed strength and hastened to the broken window in her own room. In one hand she held a lighted lamp.

"Savages! I cannot address you as gentlemen," she called to the crowd.

Astonished by her courage, they stopped. One man stood with his arm raised ready to hurl a rock; another lifted his torch above his head to get a better look at this daring Quaker woman; still another held his iron pipe like a javelin ready to be thrown. All gazed up at the silhouetted figure and listened.

"Savages, you do well to attack defenseless females who never harmed you. You are indeed brave to burn them out like a hidden enemy. Your own women must be proud of you!"

Stepping back from the window, she could hear them muttering among themselves; then slowly the figures slunk away into the night.

The next morning she and the girls counted ninety smashed windowpanes and found the paint on the house scorched.

That night of terror made Miss Crandall fearful for her brave young scholars. The school was no longer

33

1366

safe. If she repaired the house and tried to continue, marauders would surely come again.

"At best my pupils are prisoners within the walls and fence of the house and lot. Such fortifications are not strong enough," she told her father and the Reverend May with resignation.

The school disbanded, and the students left the town of Canterbury.

Opinion had run high ever since Prudence Crandall first admitted Sarah Harris to her school. Even after Miss Crandall's acquittal, Canterbury practically ostracized her, and she too finally left.

Prudence Crandall may have been forced to close her own school for black women, but her fight made possible the opening of many other schools for blacks. The episode at her school caused the repeal of the Connecticut Black Law and shook Canterbury and the county out of some of its bigotry. In the 1866 election the people of Windham County cast a large majority of votes in favor of Negro suffrage. A county historian wrote: "Miss Crandall did not succeed in teaching many colored girls, but she educated the people of Windham County."

SLAVES NO MORE

ANN WOOD

"Ann Wood, where you goin'?" Tilda, a house servant, asked the young, black ladies' maid who was tiptoeing from the feasting and dancing on the front lawn of the Wood plantation in Virginia.

Ann, only sixteen, knew Tilda was critical of her because she enjoyed the company of the field hands who were her own age. Tilda wanted Ann to remember she belonged to the big house. Usually Ann laughed at Tilda's scoldings, but today she must be careful not to annoy her.

It was Christmas Eve, 1855. The Wood slaves were dressed in their warmest clothes, faded and patched but clean. They had come to the big house for the best food they had eaten in a year, the best they would have for another year.

The story of Ann Wood is based on the historical incident of a black slave girl who led a group of other teenagers out of slavery to freedom on Christmas Eve.

Before breakfast that morning, Mistress Wood had directed, "You Nigras dig a ditch and fill it with big logs."

All morning the slaves had thrown on log after log and watched them burn down until there was a deep bed of glowing coals. They put chickens, wild turkeys, and pigs on skewers, which were laid across the searing trench. Black women kept the roasting meat turning, basting it with spicy sauces. All the time they had to keep a careful eye on the excited little ones hopping back and forth over the trenches. Tempting odors made their noses twitch and their mouths water.

A little after noon, a caravan of slaves from two neighboring plantations began arriving—some on foot, some mounted on mules. A few of the old and the very young came in carts. They were coming for the frolicking, feasting, and fiddling they had looked forward to since last Christmas. This was the one party of the year their owners allowed them.

Finally, carriages drawn by handsome purebred horses and driven by black coachmen in livery arrived. This year, as they did every Christmas, the owners of nearby plantations came to the family whose turn it was to give the annual supper for the Christmas celebrations. Watching the abandoned eating and dancing of their slaves amused and entertained the white owners.

When the owners and slaves had all arrived and the

food was on the tables, Master Wood nodded to old
Daniel, who gave the signal to Mollie. "Le's go,
everyone!" she called. Mothers lifted restraining
hands from the shoulders of the children, and young
and old swarmed to the plank tables laid out on
sawhorses under the trees.

The food steamed in the cool December air.
Besides the meats, there were hot biscuits, squash,
carrots, peach tarts, strawberry preserves, and pies—
apple, pecan, and pumpkin. Hungrily, they devoured
the delicacies. Women and men who all year long
had eaten less so their children could have more of
the scanty ration of cornmeal and bacon now ate with
abandon.

Ann Wood ate fast—a chicken drumstick, biscuits,
an apricot tart, for she always seemed to need more.
Then a rib of pork, more biscuits, and a gooseberry
tart went down. She took a turkey wing and looked
around casually as she slipped it into a burlap sack
hidden inside her blouse. Her eyes went again and
again to old Daniel, whom Master trusted to oversee
the gaieties and report if anything unusual was
happening. She hated old Daniel for the favors his
tattling won him. She kept her eyes on her master and
mistress, too. They sat on the gallery, talking with
their guests, laughing—probably at their slaves' gob-
bling of food, Ann thought bitterly. They would have
their banquet later, in the large, elegant dining room
where it was warmer. Must be tired of it all, Ann

surmised, since they were paying more attention to each other than to the feasting of their slaves.

She left the table and wove a seemingly aimless path through the scattered groups, still busy eating. At the edge of the crowded yard, she started for the stable.

"Ann Wood, where you goin'?"

She jumped at Tilda's question. "Why, I'm . . . I'm . . ." She prayed for words. "Muffin. Had her pups this mornin'. Goin' to see how she's comin'."

"Shore, shore—I forgot," Tilda muttered. She knew how Ann loved that spaniel Mrs. Wood had given her two years ago, when Ann was fourteen. Ann was Mrs. Wood's favorite personal maid. Now Tilda just laughed to herself. Her eyes followed Ann as she moved toward the barn.

What did Tilda mean by "I forgot"? Ann wondered. Forgot the pups? And why did she laugh so knowingly? Did she suspect?

Ann made herself walk slowly in case somebody did suspect and was watching her. She went into the safe darkness inside the barn and to the stall where Muffin lay with her five puppies. She leaned down to pat the dog's head and felt tears begin to form. "I'll miss you, Muff. Wish I could . . ." But she straightened up and shook off her weakness.

She walked to the rear of the barn, where the horses were stabled, and quietly slid open the back entrance. She stepped outside and pushed it closed.

Here, hidden behind the barn, was an open field cart.

"Shucks! You had me scared, Ann," young Fred said from behind the cart.

"Sh—sh! Want 'em to hear us, Fred? When'd you come in from the woods?" She felt the canvas cover Fred had put over the rickety frame of the cart. She nodded approval. "Nice, Fred. Hungry? Here." She took a turkey wing and a biscuit out of the burlap sack she pulled from her blouse and watched Fred bolt them down. She threw the sack to him. "You lay these other pickin's by the bacon slabs in the wagon. Fannie's fetchin' more."

"When we startin', Ann?"

"Hold your horses. Hear it? The fiddlin' and dancin' is beginnin'. We gotta dance—dance like we never danced before. Make 'em think we'll never stop!" Seeing Fred's disgruntled face, she drew his head close and whispered in his ear, " 'Member, 'fore mornin' we goin' to be, to be on our way. Gotta hurry back now 'fore Missus finds me gone."

Ann crept back into the barn, stopped long enough to cuddle a puppy in her hand and give it back to Muffin, ran to the front door, and moved toward the dancing.

Pete, beside Miss Lively from the Marshalls' plantation, was flying down the outside of the dancers' square and up the middle of it. He leaned back and pranced until he was exhausted. Chuck dashed in. Determined to show Lively he was better than Pete, he leaped, shuffled, and threw himself around until the set ended.

The Woods and their guests applauded from the gallery. The field hands shouted. Even the older house servants who had stayed aloof forgot their dignity and shouted, too. The fiddler's feet wouldn't stay still as his bow swung up, swung down. Those too old or too timid to join the dancing began "patting" —striking their hands on their knees, then clapping their hands together, then slapping the right shoulder with one hand and the left shoulder with the other, all the while keeping time with their feet.

Then someone started to sing and everyone joined in.

> *Goin' to the ball*
> *Feet de de dibble*
> *Who's goin' to the ball?*
> *Feet de de dibble*
> *Goin' to wear a red gown*
> *Feet de de dibble*
> *Wear a red gown*
> *Feet de de dibble*

Even the gallery folk couldn't keep still. They began to sway back and forth to the fiddler's beat and the song's "de de dibble."

Ann was stepping as high as anybody, as she and Nat jigged through the sets—in and around the oaks and back into the center of the patterns of partners.

40

Finally, while passing, she touched Fannie on the left shoulder. Fannie nodded, finished the set, and melted into the crowd. A few minutes later Ann tapped Sis. "Feelin' fine?" she questioned her as they had agreed earlier. Then she tapped Tom.

Ann and Nat danced on—first to the east, then to the west, as the fiddler called the set. She kept glancing at her mistress and Tilda and old Daniel. But none of them seemed suspicious.

During the next set, Ann excused herself to Nat and slowly walked through the revelers. Just in case Tilda was watching, she'd go to the barn by way of the big house this time. One, two, one, two, she said to herself, measuring each step. Once inside the house, the door closed, she stood panting and listening. Somebody might be in here. In the silence, she forced herself to move slowly and calmly down the wide hallway, past the open stairway. If someone chanced to glance in a window! In the dining room she dared to hurry again, into the big kitchen, where women had been baking pies and breads only a few hours ago. She paused to listen. No one.

Into the open shed behind the kitchen she went, looking around before she stepped out into the deep shadow of the house. She stayed close to the house as she crept in the direction of the barn. Between the house and the barn she had to cross a short stretch from which she could see the dancers and where they could see her.

She edged to the rim of the house shadow. "Please, God, please!" Then she walked nonchalantly into the open strip and across it. Within the blessed darkness of the barn, she turned to make sure no one had followed her. She was safe! Over the pounding of her heart, she heard the still steady pulse of fiddle, dancers, and "patters."

She knelt down and ran her hand over Muff's head. "Muff, 'bye, Muff." The cold nose nuzzled her hand.

Ann pulled herself away from her only real possession and ran to the back door, where Tom was waiting to help her with the horses.

"The others are in the cart under the canvas, you say?" she whispered. "You take Tony. Hush, Lady, it's me," she breathed into the mare's ear as she led her out by the halter. Either horse's neighing might betray them.

Silently she and Tom hitched up the horses. Ann climbed into the cart. She burrowed under the seat and brought out the weapons she had stolen and hidden over the past month. There were three double-barreled pistols and four long daggers. She gave one to each member of the group; for herself she kept a pistol and a dagger.

"Prob'bly won't need 'em, but in case . . ."

She seated herself beside Tom at the front of the cart and took the reins. "Giddap, Lady; giddap, Tony," she called softly. The wagon began moving. "We're goin'," she whispered jubilantly. "Sis, Tom,

Fannie, Fred, Nat, Ann. Goin' to the North where we're goin' to be free."

The horses klop-klopped through the meadow; the rolling wheels could carry the six of them out of slavery to freedom or capture—or death.

A dog's bark suddenly broke the night's silence. Nat crawled from the back of the wagon to behind Ann. "They set the dogs on us, Ann?"

"No, that's Muff. I know her yappin'. Tryin' to follow me." Her words were sure, but her voice was trembling with fear and a longing for her dog. Suppose someone heard Muff, investigated her whereabouts, and missed the six of them. "Nothin' to be feared of," she tried to reassure him. "But, Nat, you watch out back, just for sure . . ."

Ann drove the wagon through the dark without a word. No one spoke. The only sounds were the horses' hoofs on the road and the wheels' turning. Once a night owl's hoot made them jump. There was nothing more.

With a growing feeling of safety, Ann called back to Fannie, "Look under the straw by you. There's a map. The one Uncle Solomon made for us." She handed the reins to Tom and studied the map. She was the only one who could read it. "Gotta make Leesburg 'fore light. Robert Purvey, it says here. Ol' friend to Uncle Solomon. He'll hide us all day in his barn an' let us sleep in the hay."

The eastern sky had just begun to turn the black of

night to gray as Ann drove Tony and Lady into the Purvey yard. An hour back she'd been fighting sleep. But like a plunge into cold water, excitement at making the first station of their journey tingled through her.

"Wake up!" She roused the four sleeping figures in the wagon and jabbed her elbow into Tom, whose head was drooping.

Robert Purvey and his wife, Susan, hurried out to them and helped Ann drive into the barn. Tom and Mr. Purvey unhitched and fed the weary horses. Susan brought the young people a pail of warm milk, loaves of bread, and johnnycake with fresh-churned butter. They were hungry. Tired too, so tired that even excitement and happiness over their escape couldn't keep them awake after their stomachs were full.

They slept off and on during the day. About four-thirty, the Purveys came to tell them they must be starting to make the most of nighttime. They had to reach the second underground station, the one in Frederick, Maryland, before the following morning.

Horses and passengers were well rested, and the fugitive wagon moved off fast into the evening dusk. All felt secure. They had fooled their masters. Freedom was theirs. To the roll of the wheels through the long night, they sang songs under their breath. They changed the words of one they'd heard the old slaves sing:

Massa sleeps in the feather bed,
Nigger sleeps on the floor;
When we get to Philadelph'a
We'll be no slaves no more.

"Listen!"

"Did ya hear?"

From the distance came the beat of galloping horses and the baying of a hound.

"Someone chasin' us?"

"Sounds like it."

"Gettin' closer."

" 'Most here!"

There was no point in trying to outrun them. With the loaded wagon, poor Lady and Tony couldn't beat the hunters.

"Whoa, Lady; whoa, Tony." Ann's voice trembled. She pulled them to a halt and leaped from the cart, Nat close behind her. "Knives and guns, all of you," she commanded. "Hold the horses, Tom." She motioned Fred to get in the front seat as he started to jump down with her and Nat. "Sis and Fannie stay in the wagon."

They were hardly in their places when the five men pulled up behind them, sprang from their horses, and ran toward them. Each man carried a long rifle which he pointed at the runaways.

"Thought you were smart, eh? Thought you'd given us the slip? All the way to Maryland. Fancy

45

that!" a stranger with a sheriff's badge sneered. "Come here, you . . ." he snarled at Nat, moving toward him. "Did you hear me?"

A pistol shot sounded, and the hound fell on its side. The five men of the posse jumped involuntarily. Fred had aimed well from the front seat.

"What the—now, you son of—"

"Go ahead! Fire!" Ann dared them. The men hesitated. "Think you gonna take us? We be dead first!"

She seemed taller, stronger, than she was.

Standing beside the back of the wagon, she raised her right arm and leveled the pistol at the nearest man. Trembling with anger and fear, she lifted her left arm and waved her dagger.

The man hesitated at the sight of this bold young black woman who had the nerve to threaten him.

"Shoot! Afraid?" she dared them. She was gambling. But she knew the posse didn't want to kill them. You couldn't sell a dead slave on the market.

Nat fired a second shot. It hit one of the men in the leg.

"Well, I'll be . . . . You baggage!"

It was beginning to grow light. The knife Sis flourished from the rear of the wagon caught the first light of the sun. Fred fired again. The men backed away from the six young blacks. Ann fired her pistol into the ground at their feet. The men ran and limped to their horses.

An old engraving of Ann Wood and the other young slaves as they fought off the posse.

"We'll be back! We'll get you!" they shouted as they wheeled and sped away.

"We beat 'em. We beat 'em," Fannie said to herself as if she couldn't believe it.

Ann's legs nearly collapsed as relief coursed through her. But there wasn't time to rejoice or relax. They'd be back again with more men and rifles.

"Gotta move, fast. They'll be back. But—Maryland—we're in Maryland, did you hear them say?"

In the growing light they could see a woods, not too far off. Ann pointed to it. Fred shrugged his shoulders. No one knew what to do. They were bewildered, frightened. They turned to Ann Wood.

"Most likely hidin' place I see," she stated in a flat voice. She took her place beside Tom. "You drive, Tom. To the woods."

47

A short time later the horses were moving slowly through the woods, between the trees and through the undergrowth, on into the cover of thick evergreens which shut out the sun and made the light eerie. The boys followed behind, covering the horse and wagon tracks as best as they could.

All six, hungry and exhausted, ate the remnants of the Christmas food they had toted from the loaded tables—months ago, it seemed now. They took turns keeping guard while the other five slept and then decided to lie in their covert through the next night. Once they heard—or thought they heard—hoof beats.

The second evening after their triumph over the posse, Ann drove the field cart out into open country.

"Headin' for Frederick. We'll get there by mornin'," she announced as she traced their route on the map with her finger.

To the wagon's jolting rhythm, the refugees sang softly, "We'll be no slaves no more."

Stations of the Underground Railroad harbored them in Frederick and Hagarstown, Maryland, and in Hanover, New Providence, Coatsville and Conshohocken, Pennsylvania.

Three weeks after their flight from the plantation, Ann Wood drove the faithful horses into Philadelphia. The six young blacks were as skittery as the horses at the noise and bustle of the big city. Here, by arrangement through underground "conductors," they were met by Thomas Garret, a white Quaker, and William Still, a free Negro.

"And Ann dared them to fire at you?" their listeners marveled that first evening in Philadelphia. "Astonishing! But who planned the scheme for you to get away?"

"Ann Wood," Nat promptly volunteered.

"And she directed you between stations?"

"Shore did," Fred grunted.

"Not me, not me alone," Ann interrupted. "Uncle Solomon and Fannie's ma and Jen—didn't want us sold. Like they had been. Risked whippin' or worse to help us all slip out. And all of you. Now, thank God, we're here, safe in Philadelphia. Wish they could know."

Softly Ann Wood began singing and the other five joined her in their own hymn of freedom:

> *Here in Philadelph'a*
> *We'll be no slaves no more.*

ALIEN DAUGHTERS

SARAH AND ANGELINA GRIMKÉ

The behavior and ideas of Sarah and Angelina Grimké were becoming more and more disturbing to their parents.

Judge John Faucherand Grimké and Mary Smith Grimké were descendants of the early settlers of South Carolina. Southern aristocrats, they owned plantations, a large home in Charleston, and many slaves. She was a leader of Charleston society and of the Episcopal church. He was a member of the South Carolina Supreme Court. Both accepted the Southern way of life as the natural and right way to live.

They gave their two daughters the usual education for future belles of Charleston—handwork, music, a bit of French, and, above all, the social graces.

They knew both Sarah and Angelina idolized their older brother, Thomas, who had studied law and, to

Judge and Mrs. Grimké's dismay, had declared slavery an evil. He talked too much to his sisters about his ideas for reform, and they listened to him. His early death in 1834 deepened his influence on them. They too became rebels against the Southern way of life.

They cut the lace and trimmings from their dresses and even the bows from their shoes; destroyed the family set of Scott's novels, which they called "sentimental indulgence"; persuaded their mother to give daily religious instruction to all the slaves; and reprimanded her for indulging in such "luxury and ease" as having the drawing room repapered.

Sarah shocked them by wanting to attend law school as Thomas did; and Angelina, after witnessing the beating of a family slave, ran to a local sea captain, "Captain, take Ticey away on your ship. Where no one can whip her anymore."

"What's gotten into Sarah and Angelina?" Mrs. Grimké asked her husband. "Fancy two pretty young girls with such deep blue eyes! And long curls! They could be the belles of Charleston! But what do they do? Worry about Ticey. Angelina refusing to be confirmed because she says the church shouldn't favor slavery! What can we do about them?"

Judge Grimké sighed and shook his head.

No wonder their parents called these two girls their "alien daughters."

Although Sarah was thirteen years older than

Portrait by Pierre Henri of Mary Smith Grimké, the mother of Sarah and Angelina. Carolina Art Association of the Gibbes Art Gallery, Charleston, South Carolina

Angelina, the two sisters followed the same pattern of revolt and reform.

The child Angelina wept when she heard slaves cry in pain after lashings. She hid ointment in her own room. When the household was asleep, Angelina would creep down the stairs and tiptoe to the slave quarters to rub the healing oil into the open wounds.

Both girls deliberately disobeyed the South Carolina law which made the teaching of any slave to read illegal. Sarah started to teach her own slave girl but was stopped when Judge Grimké discovered his daughter's defiance.

Angelina, when she was old enough, also taught her dressing maid to read. Her method escaped detection. In the diary which was to be her constant confidante, she recorded: "The light was put on, the keyhole screened, and flat on our stomachs before the fire, we defied the laws of South Carolina."

Once when Judge Grimké went to Philadelphia, he

took Sarah with him. There she met some Quakers who impressed her so much that, after her father's death, she became a Quaker. She was one of three in the entire city of Charleston—two old men and herself. In her simple Quaker costume, she walked the city's Battery among the Southern ladies. She was a visible sign of dissent and of revolt against the life to which she had been born.

The two sisters could not tolerate for long the conditions they believed unjust and wrong. Angelina described the condition of house slaves as bad—sleeping on bare floors, receiving only two meals a day and often deprived of one or both as punishment. She cringed as she heard the familiar whir of the whip followed by cries of anguish.

Twenty-seven-year-old Sarah, visiting Quaker friends in Philadelphia, decided to break from her Charles-

An old engraving of a slave-coffle. Library of Congress

ton life and remain in the North. Angelina, still too young to leave, continued to live at home for some years. She struggled unsuccessfully against her family's role in slavery—tried to persuade her mother to stand with her against slavery, begged her brother Henry to be merciful to his slaves.

A visit to Philadelphia was a turning point in Angelina's life. Here in Pennsylvania, she sensed freedom for all. By 1830, Pennsylvania, like the other states north of the Mason-Dixon line, had passed antislavery laws. In 1825, Pennsylvania passed "personal liberty" laws to protect free Negroes from being returned to slavery. Angelina felt the contrast when she returned to Charleston. She wrote in her diary, "Must it not be laid down as an axiom, that that system is radically wrong which can be supported only by trespassing the laws of God?" Shortly after, because of frustration at her helplessness in the midst of slavery, she made the open break.

She wrote in a letter to Sarah, "I cannot but be pained at the thought of leaving mother. . . . I do not think, dear sister, I will ever see her again until she is willing to give up slavery." That autumn, 1829, Angelina, then twenty-five, left Charleston. She never did see her mother again.

In Philadelphia, the Grimké sisters began to discover flaws even in the Quakers, to whom Sarah and Angelina seemed like rebels. They refused to use some of the archaic forms of Quaker speech; they insisted on wearing their own style of bonnet; they prayed aloud into the silence of Quaker meetings. Most of all, they disputed with the Quakers about slavery and insisted on sitting during meetings in the section assigned to black women. "While you put this badge of degradation on our sisters, we feel it is our duty to share it with them." After a time of inner searching, they broke with the Quakers, principally because of their position on slavery.

In 1835, Angelina wrote a letter to the abolitionist William Lloyd Garrison. "It is my deep, solemn, deliberate conviction that this [abolition of slavery] is a cause worth dying for. . . ." She apologized for disturbing so busy a man but said she could not resist writing him who stood "in the forefront of the battle." Each week, she told him, she opened his paper *The Liberator* fearing he might in some way have compromised or retreated. But she had gradually gained confidence that nothing could move him, not even physical assault. "The ground upon which you stand is holy ground." After days of hesitation and prayer, she sent the letter to Garrison.

Delighted with the tribute to him, Garrison welcomed her to the cause. He said of Angelina's letter: "Its spirit, dignity, faith, devotion are such as have never been excelled by the noblest exhibition of Christian martyrdom even since the days of the apostles." He could not resist publishing it in *The Liberator*.

Sarah Moore Grimké

The letter brought Angelina to the fore of the abolitionist movement. In Charleston, South Carolina, Angelina and Garrison were listed as the number-one enemies of the South.

Many Quakers had come to favor colonization of the blacks in Liberia over abolition of slavery in the States. They urged her to join them. Sarah too at this point questioned her sister's stand.

Instead, Angelina wrote a thirty-six-page pamphlet called "An Appeal to Christian Women of the South." Calling slavery "a whited sepulchre, full of dead men's bones and all uncleanness," it delighted abolitionists and enraged slave owners. In it she pleaded with all Southern women to fight slavery, "this horrible system of oppression and cruelty, licentiousness and wrong." She begged them "to read, to pray, to act." Free the slaves and seek their education even if in so doing you break the law.

In South Carolina the pamphlet was called the "ravings of a fanatic." It caused an uproar, and the Charleston postmaster burned copies in the public square.

Not long after its publication, Angelina's mother received a visit from the mayor.

He rose as she swept into the reception room. "This meeting, Mrs. Grimké, causes me great pain. I regret embarrassing you." He paused, then plunged on. "I have learned that your daughter, Miss Angelina, author of this pamphlet . . ."

"Yes?"

"That she is planning to come to Charleston to visit you." The mayor lost his tone of apology as he continued, "You must inform your daughter that if she comes into this port, the police have instructions to prevent her leaving the boat. They are to see that she does not communicate by letter or otherwise with anyone in the city."

"And if she does?"

"If she should elude the officers and come ashore, Madam, we shall arrest her and detain her in prison until the vessel returns. And may I add that for her own safety, for your safety, she must not come. There are many threats of violence against her."

"Mr. Mayor!"

"You will so inform her?"

"Yes. Of course. Oh, Angelina . . ." Her voice trailed off. "Yes, indeed I must," the mother, confused and outraged by her heretic daughter, promised.

"Good day, Madam."

Angelina, for the sake of her family, unwillingly gave up her visit to Charleston, but she was not silenced. A year later she published another pamphlet, "An Epistle to the Clergy of the Southern States." This upbraided ministers for supporting, or at least not opposing, degradation of human beings through slavery.

Sarah was now in full sympathy with Angelina. Both were widely known. The secretary of the American Antislavery Society invited them to the state of New York to speak to women abolitionists. As a team, they launched their career as evangelists of abolition.

In New York and New England, which they made their home base, they held parlor meetings, so-called because they were scheduled for parlors in private homes. The Grimké name was not on the meeting notices, but word spread. Once, as many as three hundred women tried to crowd into one parlor, and the meeting had to be moved to a nearby Baptist church. This was probably one of the first times that an American woman had ever addressed a public meeting in a public hall.

A man came to one of these meetings. Angelina noted in her diary, "Somehow, I did not feel his presence embarrassing at all and went on just as though he had not been there."

Men longed to hear these exciting women with their firsthand knowledge of slavery—their tales of children driven through the streets of Charleston on their way to New Orleans to be sold. Two men slipped into the back seats of another meeting. At still another, men barred from entering stood on ladder rungs outside and listened through open windows. In Dorchester, Massachusetts, men boldly entered the town hall and took seats.

That a woman should speak to a mixed audience was thought "unscriptural" and stirred violent opposition among opponents of abolition and women's rights. The sisters' speaking provoked such protest that they took on the cause of women's rights as well as abolition. Sarah, in a pamphlet called "Letters on the Equality of the Sexes and the Condition of Women," said, "The pages of history teem with woman's wrongs; it is wet with woman's tears." She urged women to "plant themselves beside men to whom they were designed to be companions and helpers in every good word and work."

Such statements fanned the opposition. In Groton, Massachusetts, a gang of boys pelted the sisters with apples. In Boston, every church was closed to them and placards announcing meetings in private homes were torn down. A Congregational clergyman in

Worcester threatened to resign if Angelina was allowed to speak in his parish house. The General Association of Congregational Ministers of Massachusetts condemned the sisters in a tirade against women who preached and tried to reform. The newspapers named them Devilina and Grimalkin.

They were satirized in verse:

> *They've taken a notion to speak for them-*
> *selves,*
> *And are wedding the tongue and the pen;*
> *They've mounted the rostrum, the termagant*
> *elves,*
> *And–oh, horrid!–are talking to men.*

In spite of the ridicule and protest, they held their meetings, and women and men flocked to them. Sometimes two halls had to be rented in a town. Angelina spoke in one and Sarah in the other. The audiences sang the hymns of abolition, "I Am an Abolitionist—I Glory in the Name" and "Freedom's Summons."

In Boston, they spoke for six successive nights at the Odeon Theater to audiences of two to three thousand. Their voices were hoarse from exhaustion. Angelina's entry in her diary shows how tired they were: "I am sometimes so sick before I rise that it seems almost impossible for me to speak ten minutes." But speak she did, fervently, for an hour or more.

Wendell Phillips, a leading abolitionist, said her eloquence "swept the chords of the human heart with a power that has never been surpassed and rarely equaled. I well remember, evening after evening, listening to eloquence such as had never been heard from a woman."

Angelina, the better speaker of the two, had her greatest triumph when she spoke to the Massachusetts legislature in 1838. Before, no woman had ever been heard in these halls. One report has it that the room was so packed that she had to be passed over the heads of the spectators to reach the platform. On the second day an antagonistic legislator sought to stop the meeting with the excuse that the huge crowds threatened the safety of the gallery. Another legislator, from Salem, said a committee should be appointed to examine the foundation of the State House to see whether it would bear another lecture from Miss Grimké.

To her diary Angelina confessed, "My heart never quailed before, but it almost died within me at that hour." Outwardly she appeared calm and indifferent to the judgment of those around her, as she stood before the spellbound legislators of the Commonwealth of Massachusetts.

"I stand before you as a Southerner exiled from the land of my birth by the sounds of the lash, and the piteous cry of the slave. I stand before you as a repentant slaveholder. I stand before you as a moral

Angelina Grimké

being . . . as a moral being I owe it to the suffering
slave and to the deluded master, to my country and
the world, to do all that I can to overturn a system of
complicated crimes, built up upon the broken hearts
and prostrate bodies of my countrymen in chains and
cemented by the blood and sweat and tears of my
sisters in bonds."

Angelina knew she had spoken well and confided
her delight to her diary. "The chairman was in tears
almost the whole time I was speaking."

When the two sisters had first begun their evangel-
izing, they needed training in lecturing. They went to
Theodore Weld, a Connecticut abolitionist. He
quickly recognized Angelina's superiority as a speaker
and advised Sarah to concentrate on writing.

Out of courtesy, he often accompanied the sisters
to meetings. As he discovered his courtesy turning to
love for Angelina, he held back, determined to avoid
any entanglements which might interfere with his
antislavery mission. He would not let himself even
take her arm as they proceeded to a lecture. Poor
Angelina, already in love, did not dare to hope. Their
devotion to a common cause, it may be, finally let

him express his love, and in May of 1838 they were married.

Their wedding was no ordinary wedding. They made it a demonstration for antislavery and woman's rights. Angelina and Theodore invited six former Grimké slaves as "our protest against the horrible prejudice." Two Negro and two white clergymen were there to offer prayers. According to a Pennsylvania law, a marriage was legal if witnessed by twelve people. William Lloyd Garrison read the marriage agreement with Angelina and Theodore officiating. Weld read an attack against "the unrighteous power vested in a husband by laws of the United States over the person and property of his wife."

Boycotting sugar from cane cultivated and cut by slave labor, they had the wedding cake made with "free" sugar. "The mattress for our farm home in New Jersey," Angelina insisted, "is not to be made with the usual slave-grown cotton ticking."

Their honeymoon was devoted to the cause. The Welds attended the opening of the Antislavery Convention of American Women in the new sumptuous, gas-lit Pennsylvania Hall.

On the first night of the convention, there were three thousand Negro and white delegates seated together—a defiance of social custom. This unprecedented mingling of whites and blacks drew a mob outside the hall. They threw stones at the windows, shouted, and jeered.

For nearly an hour, Angelina, a bride of two days, addressed the audience, interrupted by hootings, stones, and stamping. One delegate said Angelina was not surpassed in courage and consecration by Paul among the wild beasts at Ephesus.

She talked above the confusion: "Men, brothers, mothers, daughters, sisters . . . I am here as a Southerner to perform my duty of bearing testimony against slavery. I have seen it—I have known its horrors, which can never be described. I witnessed for many years its demoralizing influence and its destructiveness of human happiness." Shouts and insults made her pause to be heard. She continued: "Many accept that the slave is unhappy under the worst forms of slavery. But I have *never* seen a happy slave. I have seen him dance in his chains, it is true; but he is not happy." There were more shouts and insults. That slaves were sometimes mirthful, she conceded. "With all hope gone, they adopt the attitude, 'Let us eat, drink, for tomorrow we die'. . . .

"In slavery there is no neutral ground. If you are not for it, you must be against it. . . .

"What can we do? We can show the mob with its threats that we are unafraid, are ready to die for the cause. . . .

"And what can we women who have no voice at the ballot box do? It is peculiarly your duty to petition," she adjured them. If enough women circulate petitions and write to their legislators, she prophesied, they will respond. "When the maids and matrons of the land are knocking at our doors, we must legislate." The South, Angelina said, would pale before the numbers of petitions.

The following night a mob of fifteen thousand besieged the hall. While the mayor was there, they listened to his appeal to refrain from violence. But after he left and the meeting adjourned, the hecklers broke into the building and burned it to the ground.

After the convention, to recover from their exhaustion, the Welds and Sarah Grimké retired to New Jersey and later to Massachusetts, their permanent home. Although they remained active in other ways, they did very little public speaking.

Theodore Weld and his sister-in-law Sarah studied thousands of papers carrying advertisements for fugitive slaves and asked other opponents of slavery to send them any advertisements they found. The following descriptions of runaways were common: "will no doubt show marks of recent whippings," "stamped on the left cheek *R* and a piece is taken off her left ear," "branded *N.E.* on the breast and having both small toes cut off." Without fear of any stigma, white owners put their full names and addresses to such advertisements.

A great antislavery tract, "Slavery As It Is: The Testimony of a Thousand Witnesses," was the result.

It was so revealing that Harriet Beecher Stowe is said to have had it in her sewing basket by her all the time she was writing *Uncle Tom's Cabin.*

The Grimké sisters had occasion to practice their antislavery creed. One day Angelina chanced to read in a paper that a young Negro man was to speak at Lincoln University in Pennsylvania. The man's name was Archibald Grimké. Wondering at the coincidence, she immediately investigated and found there were two brothers there, Archibald and Francis. Upon further inquiry, the sisters learned the boys were indeed their nephews. After his wife's death, their brother Henry, of Charleston, had a Negro slave, Nancy Webster, come as a nurse for his children. These two boys were the sons of Henry and Nancy.

Angelina and Sarah publicly acknowledged their black nephews and made them members of the Weld–Grimké household. At the expense of their aunts, Archibald and Francis completed their education, Francis at Princeton Theological Seminary and Archibald at Harvard Law School. The aunts challenged the boys to set the name of Grimké once more "among the princes of our land." They had good cause to be proud of these black nephews. Francis became pastor of the Fifteenth Street Presbyterian Church in Washington, D.C., and Archibald became U.S. Consul to Santo Domingo and vice-president of the newly founded NAACP.

66

The secretary of the American Antislavery Society said of Sarah and Angelina Grimké: "The Lord has opened a wide door of usefulness to these two sisters. Wherever they go they awaken a deep and powerful interest for the suffering slave."

Daughters of wealthy slave holders, guilt-ridden by the system their family and friends defended, these rebel women renounced their heritage and journeyed to the North, where they preached the Gospel of Abolition. By their personal witness, they fired the conscience of many American men and women.

JOURNEY INTO FREEDOM

WILLIAM AND ELLEN CRAFT

He clipped off the last lock of her long black hair. In the darkness they embraced before kneeling and praying for guidance and protection. As they rose, William took Ellen's hand. Together they crept softly to the door. Gently, oh so gently, he raised the latch, pushed the door open a crack. They peered out and listened. Even the trees around the hut stood silent.

"Come, my dearest, come," William whispered. For a moment they stood outside, waiting. They took a step. "My love, our first step toward freedom."

Ellen shrank back. He put his arms around her. She laid her head on his breast and sobbed. Sobbed without a sound. No man or woman, slave or free, must detect them. "No, I can't. I thought I could but—"

"Hush, Ellen. We can!" He smiled as he looked her up and down. "A fine young gentleman like you in a stovepipe hat, trousers, cutaway coat. With his slave boy."

She shuddered as she looked down at her man's clothing but managed to smile back. She straightened her shoulders. "Come, William, I'm ready."

He locked the hut door, turning the key as if he were locking away their past. Hardly daring to breathe for fear of waking Ellen's mistress, they tiptoed across the lawn. They kissed without a word and walked in different directions to the depot.

Three evenings earlier, William Craft had come from the shop where his master rented out his services as a cabinetmaker. Allowed to keep for himself a fraction of the money his cabinets earned for his master, William had managed to accumulate quite a tidy sum.

"I have the perfect plan!" Exultantly, he unfolded his scheme to Ellen, his wife.

She was personal maid to her second mistress. Her first mistress had hated Ellen because the girl was her husband's daughter by a slave and so light that she could pass for white. She was often taken for a daughter of the family. So her mistress gave the slave child as a wedding gift to her own daughter. With this second family, Ellen, then only eleven, went to Macon, Georgia.

There she met William, a black lad apprenticed by his master to a cabinetmaker. For several years, they postponed asking permission to marry. Ellen had seen too many children torn from their mothers to wish to bear any. Instead, they discussed various plans for escape.

But the difficulties seemed insurmountable. No public conveyance would take a slave or, for that matter, a free Negro, unless he had positive proof of his freedom. Bloodhounds were put on the scent of runaways. To William and Ellen the distance of some one thousand miles across slave states seemed endless.

Finally they decided to get their two owners' permission to marry and to settle down in slavery. They were as comfortable as slaves could be under a system where they were chattels. Yet they never quite sank into accepting it. Again and again one dreamed a plan of escape and confided it to the other only to discover its impossibility.

Ellen's response to William's perfect plan was one of disbelief.

"Listen to me! You're tall, slender. And you can pass for white! I'll buy, collect, steal clothes for you! It's December 18. At Christmas, our masters will give us passes for a few days' absence. Once on the train, we'll travel together, you as my white master and I as your slave boy."

"As your mistress, you mean."

"No! No white woman'd travel alone with a black boy."

"But, William, it's too far! And where'll we stay?"

"At the best hotels, my master. With the money I've saved." He bowed and kissed her hand.

"You forget." Tears of rage swam in her eyes. "As I do her hair, Mistress often says to me, 'What should I do without you, Ellen, my favorite?' But she has never taught me to read and write. No, without that, we can never do it!"

"We'll manage. You speak like an educated white; you look like an aristocratic Southerner. But the writing . . ."

Suddenly Ellen took a key from her apron pocket and went to the handsome cabinet that had been William's wedding present to her. Her mistress let Ellen keep it in the one-room cabin she had given her slave when the girl married. Ellen unlocked a drawer and took out a large scarf her mistress had tired of. She folded it and made it into a sling for her right arm.

"William, boy. I suffer from severe rheumatism, so acute I can't use my right hand."

They hugged each other and laughed silently. No one must overhear their amusement. William fondled her face.

"Your skin's too smooth. Not a man's," he said.

Ellen began weeping. Again they had let themselves dream fantasies.

"Wait, I'll make a poultice," she smiled. "Put it in a white handkerchief under my chin, up around my cheeks and tie it over my head." She matched her words with the fastening of a bandana. "See, skin and face nearly hidden."

She looked at herself in the little clouded mirror over the cabinet. "My eyes—they're scared-looking. Spectacles, dark spectacles! Buy me a pair. And my voice. Listen." She spoke in a low tone—deep for a woman, light for a man. But it would pass.

All that night of December 18, 1848, William and Ellen Craft lay on the narrow cot and talked, schemed until an hour before dawn when they must go about their master's and mistress' business.

During the next three days, William bought the needed items, each at a different store to avoid suspicion. They secured passes from their owners for a few days before Christmas—passes they could not read. They felt jubilant: they had overlooked nothing; no one suspected.

And tonight they kissed and began their separate journeys to the depot.

Once there, Ellen, inwardly quaking, outwardly bold, stepped up to the ticket window. "To Savannah—one for me, one for my boy." She motioned to the platform where William was standing.

With the two tickets in hand, she went into one of the best carriages and told William to go to a rear car. Taking a seat by the window, she nearly panicked

An old engraving of Ellen Craft dressed as a young slaveholder.

as she saw William's cabinetmaster talking to the ticket agent. He was gesturing frantically toward the train and then he jumped on. He stepped inside Ellen's coach and glanced around. She kept her head turned away, held her breath, and gazed out the window. He headed to the back cars, passed Ellen's seat but did not stop. He could not fail to recognize William! Fortunately, before he reached William's car, the bell rang, the train crept into motion, and she saw him leap from the train steps. She could breathe again.

In the meantime, someone had sat down beside Ellen. It was Mr. Gray, an old friend of her master. In fact he had dined with the family only the day before. Fear of detection pulsed through her.

"It's a very fine morning, sir," Gray said to the young man seated beside him.

Terrified, Ellen pretended deafness and took no notice.

Gray raised his voice. "I say, it's a very fine morning, sir."

Still no response. A passenger laughed.

"I'll make him hear." Gray shouted, "It is, indeed, a very fine morning, sir."

Ellen turned her head slightly, bowed politely. "Yes." Again she watched the passing landscape.

"Great deprivation to be deaf," another passenger observed to Mr. Gray.

"Yes, I shall trouble that fellow no more."

To her relief the conversation turned to topics of major interest to Georgia gentlemen—slaves, cotton, and those Yankee abolitionists. Ellen had heard the word, abolitionist, in her master's house. Wild animals, she had thought it meant then. But according to what they were saying here, "those cutthroat abolitionists" were friends of runaway slaves like herself and William.

At the town of Gordon, many people, including Mr. Gray, left for a change of train.

In the early evening Ellen and William's train reached Savannah. An omnibus met the train to take the passengers to the steamboat bound for Charleston, South Carolina.

When they arrived, Ellen went directly to her

cabin pretending to be suffering from extreme rheumatism. She had her "boy" William bring her luggage there, then sent him to heat up the flannels and ointment.

After he had made Ellen as comfortable as he could for the night, William approached the steward. "Whar ah sleep?" he asked with a heavy accent.

The steward shrugged his shoulders. "No special place for niggers, slave or free."

William paced the deck, then climbed on some cotton bags piled near the ship's funnel. It was warm there till very late. He curled up and tried to sleep. But he was too tense. For the few hours before going to help his "master" get ready for the day, he sweated through nightmares of flight and capture.

At breakfast in the dining room, "Master" Ellen was seated at the right of the ship's captain. All were solicitous of her health. Her "boy" cut the food for her, since her right arm in its sling was useless.

As William left, the captain observed, "A very attentive boy you have, sir. Better watch him like a hawk up North. He's very safe here, but may be mighty different there."

"Sound doctrine, Captain, very sound," said a slave dealer with a Yankee accent, his thumbs in his vestholes, his mouth full of chicken. "I wouldn't take a nigger to the North under no consideration. Never saw one that had his heels on free soil that was worth a damn." The trader turned directly to Ellen. "Now, stranger, if you want to sell that boy, just mention your price. I'll pay for him with hard silver dollars. What you say, stranger?"

"I don't wish to sell, sir. How could I get on without him?" She pointed with her left hand to the sling and poultice.

"You'll learn to get along without him. He's a keen one, and I see from his eyes he's sure to run away."

"I'm sure not, sir. I know his fidelity." She managed to keep her voice steady.

"Fidevil! What you saying? There ain't one of 'em wouldn't run away, given the chance."

Forcing herself to ignore the slave trader, Ellen thanked the captain for his advice. She strolled on deck for a while. Then she told a fellow passenger that she found the air too keen for her rheumatism and returned to the safety of her cabin.

But at the door, she found a young military officer who had been on the train the previous day and also at the table this morning.

"Excuse me, sir," the officer advised Ellen, "but I think you're spoiling your boy by saying 'thank you' to him. Only way to keep a nigger in his place is to storm at him like thunder, keep him trembling like a leaf. If he was drilled that way, he'd be as humble as a dog and never dare run away." He added, "Foolish of you to go north for your health. Go to Hot Springs, Arkansas."

"No, I think the air of Philadelphia will suit my

complaint best. Besides, I can get better medical advice there, I've been told."

Despite these encounters, both Ellen and William dreaded leaving the boat, which now seemed a kind of haven to them. They worried that William's cabinet-making master might have gone to their owners and that they might be caught when they docked in Charleston.

Reluctantly, they walked down the gangplank with the last of the passengers. William helped the limping Ellen. He summoned a cab and directed the cabman to take them to the best hotel.

There, the landlord treated Ellen as a gentleman of high position. He even helped the young invalid into the lobby. "You take the other arm," he snapped at William. Then he signed the register for the gentleman and gave him one of the best rooms. "Run to the kitchen. Have the cook make two poultices right off. Hurry, boy! Your master's badly off."

Once in the room, William helped his wife get rid of her sling and poultice. What a relief! She snatched off the spectacles, worked her arm up and down and bathed her face in cool water. She kissed her husband gleefully. So far, so good. Exhausted from the strain of the trip, she stretched out on the wide bed, while William took her boots down for polishing by Pompey, a slave in the hotel.

"Say, brudder, way you from? Way you goin' wid your fine massa?" Pompey asked.

"To Philadelphia."

"I wish I was goin' wid you! I hears um say dere's no slaves in dem parts. Is dat so?"

"I've heard so."

Pompey swung around and looked long at William. "God bless you, brudder. May de Lord be wid you."

William carried the boots back to Ellen, and again they put on the disguise of invalidism. They went into the elegant dining room shining with silver and crystal, where William cut the food for his "master's" dinner. In the kitchen he was given scraps on a broken plate with rusty knife and fork. "Here, boy, see that you stay in the kitchen," he was told.

The next morning, they went for tickets to the custom-house office near the wharf where their boat for Wilmington, North Carolina, was docked.

"Sign your name and your nigger's. You pay a dollar duty on him," the ticket agent told Ellen. To William, "Boy, do you belong to this gentleman?"

"Yes, sir."

"Will you please sign my name," Ellen asked the agent. "I'm crippled, you see."

"You'll sign your name and your boy's, too, if you take him on board. I'm running no risks."

The young military officer who had been on the boat emerged from the crowd that was watching the altercation. Ellen and William had not liked him and his advice. Now, however, he was their savior.

Portrait of William Craft

"I know this gentleman and will vouch for him. I will register the gentleman's name and take responsibility upon myself." The ticket seller, who knew the officer, turned with relief to pick up the register. The officer murmured, "Your name?"

"William Johnson."

"Mr. Johnson and one slave," the officer wrote.

The ticket agent glanced at the names and let the two take the boat for the day's journey to Wilmington.

The following day, which was the fourth day of their trip, they boarded the train carrying them from Wilmington to Richmond, Virginia. Because of "Master" Ellen's invalid state, she was given an apartment with a couch at the end of one car. An elderly Southern gentleman and his two daughters shared it.

"What is your illness?" he asked.

"Inflammatory rheumatism. My father is sending me to Philadelphia for better medical treatment than I can get in Georgia."

"I sympathize. I have suffered from it too and know how painful it is. You had best lie down."

The two daughters offered their shawls to the invalid. William arranged them as a pillow and carefully covered his "master" with the older man's coat.

"I reckon your master's father hasn't any smarter and more faithful boy than you," he commented to William.

"Oh, yes, he has, sir. Lots of 'em."

He gave William a ten-cent piece. "Now see that you're attentive to your good master."

Thinking Ellen asleep, one daughter said, "Papa, he seems to be such a nice young gentleman!"

"Oh, dear me," the other daughter added, "I never felt so much for a gentleman in my whole life!"

In spite of his fear that their admiring friends might discover the hoax, William could hardly keep from laughing. Ellen pretended to be fast asleep.

Just before they left the train at Richmond, the kindly father wrote a cure for Ellen's inflammatory rheumatism. With it, he gave her his card and said, "I shall be pleased to see you at my home. And so will my daughters, good sir."

She thanked them. Almost too hastily she folded

the paper with the card inside and slipped them into her pocket, fearing that the fact she could read neither one would be evident.

The train would take them from Richmond to Washington, and from Washington to Baltimore, the last town of any note before Pennsylvania, free territory.

Saturday morning, December 24, they were at the Baltimore depot. They changed trains, and after settling his "master" in the coach, William hurried for the back car where he was to travel. A ticket agent halted him.

"Where you going, boy?"

"To Philadelphia, sir."

"Well, what you going there for?"

"I'm trav'lin' with my massa, in nex' carriage, sir."

"You'd better get out. Quick, boy! No slave on this train going from slave to free territory unless his master can prove his right to take you. Hurry, boy, train's leaving soon."

William ran back to Ellen, who smiled at him with new confidence and risked an elated whisper. "By five tomorrow morning—Philadelphia!"

As William told her the agent's demands, her smile faded. She would have to brave the agent, they decided. It was their only chance.

As the agent entered their car, Ellen mustered her assurance. "You wish to see me, sir?" she asked.

"Yes, sir." His manner was brusque. "No slaves let

through from Baltimore to Philadelphia without proof of the master's ownership."

"And why is that?"

"Supposin' that boy"—he pointed to William—"wasn't rightfully yours and his real master came after we'd let him through. We'd have to pay for him. That's why."

"But I have tickets from Charleston to Philadelphia for myself and my boy. The ownership papers are at my home. I was sick and left in a hurry. You have no right to detain me!"

"Well, sir, right or wrong, I shan't let you through without those papers. Unless you know some gentleman in Baltimore to vouch that this boy is yours."

Ellen was so terrified she didn't dare say more for fear her voice might give her away.

Some of the passengers began to sympathize with the young man who was obviously a cripple and not at all well.

"Oh, look at him. He's all right."

"Let him through."

The bell rang warning of the train's departure.

"Come on, officer." The passengers were edgy. They wanted to get moving.

"Don't quite know what I ought to do." The officer hesitated. "Calculate it's all right this time," he said grudgingly and told a clerk to have the conductor let the gentleman and his slave pass.

Weak from relief, Ellen let William settle her in

the coach. Then he raced back to his car as the train pulled out for Philadelphia.

Nothing could stop them now!

William had slept very little in the last five days. Now, all alone in the car and confident at last, he relaxed and slept on the last lap of his journey into freedom.

At Havre de Grace, special ferry boats took all passengers across the Susquehanna River, where they boarded another train. All passengers, that is, except those traveling in the carriage allotted to slaves.

William slept so soundly he knew nothing of these changes.

In her coach "Master" Ellen waited as long as she dared for her "boy." For the first time since they had left Macon, he was not there to help her.

"Conductor, have you seen my slave?"

"No, sir. Probably ran away. In Philadelphia by now. Free."

"Won't you please see if you can find him?"

"I'm no slave hunter. Everybody, as far as I'm concerned, has to look after their own niggers."

What could she do? She had no money; they had put all they had into William's pocket, knowing that it was the last place anyone would look. Maybe William had been kidnapped back into slavery. But she did have the tickets. Her wisest course, she decided, was to board the ferry and go on to Philadelphia and from there try to trace William.

The car where William was sleeping and the baggage car behind it were rolled onto a freight ferry. Once across the river, the two cars were attached to the train Ellen was on.

Exhausted, William did not wake until the train began to pull out and a conductor screamed at him, "Boy, wake up! Your master's scared half to death about you. Never in my life saw a fellow so scared about losing his slave!"

"Why?"

"Thinking you've run away!" The trainman lowered his voice. "And if I was you, when you get to Philadelphia, leave that cripple and take your liberty."

Another trainman whispered to him, "There's a boarding house I know in Philadelphia. Run by an abolitionist who takes in colored folks from the South."

He told William the address. William kept repeating the name of the street and the number to himself as the train moved on into Pennsylvania.

The whistle of the steam engine pierced the dawn, and William pushed up the window and stuck out his head. He saw a conductor leap to the station platform before the train came to a stop. He heard him shout the welcome word, "Phil-a-DEL-phia."

William dashed forward to Ellen and helped her off. The invalid leaned on him as he called a cab and gave the address he had memorized.

For the first time in days, he cast off his role and got into the cab and sat with his wife. "Ellen! Can you believe it? We're here! Free! Thank God!"

Through a wealthy Negro in Philadelphia, they went to a farm owned by Quakers. When Ellen realized they were white, not passing for white like her, she was terrified that they might sell them back into slavery. Slowly their kindness won her trust. From them, after each evening meal, Ellen and William had their first lessons in reading and writing. Soon they could spell and write their names quite legibly.

On advice from Philadelphia friends, Ellen and William went on to Boston. There, they became independent and self-supporting, William as a cabinetmaker and furniture broker and Ellen as a seamstress. Self-supporting and active in the abolitionist movement, they knew the happiness of free people for nearly two years.

Then, one day in October of 1850, William entered the room where Ellen sat hemming the ballgown she was finishing for her patron. His long silence made her look up.

"William, what is it?"

"Again, Ellen. They're after us again. Your master and mistress and my master." His voice broke. "They've sent agents, two of them, to get us."

"But they can't... Here? In Boston? They can't."

"Oh, yes, they can. The Fugitive Slave Act. Remember? They've discussed it at the abolition meetings in Faneuil Hall. It allows the government to take slaves back to their masters by force from anywhere in the United States. Even in free territory. That's what's happening to us."

For nearly two weeks they were hunted by these agents with writs against the two of them. They tried to get William by accusing him of stealing.

Theodore Parker, a Boston clergyman who was also an abolitionist and leader of the Boston Vigilance Committee, promptly took steps to protect the fugitives. He and his wife hid Ellen in their home and saw that William was also hidden and well armed. Parker led a successful campaign to terrify the slave catchers into leaving the city.

A Whig offered to buy both Ellen and William from their owners and give them their legal freedom if they would let themselves be arrested. As representatives of three hundred or more fugitive slaves in Boston, the Crafts refused.

The whole episode heightened the slave fervor in the South. The Crafts' former masters appealed to President Fillmore and had his promise of their return to Georgia. He sent a military force to Boston to assure their capture.

In view of the increasing threat to William and Ellen Craft's freedom, Theodore Parker and other abolitionists arranged their flight from Boston. Before they left, however, Mr. Parker performed a legal, if hasty, marriage ceremony for them. In Georgia, they had had only a slave wedding, which was meaningless before the law.

Directly after the wedding, their abolitionist friends hustled them from Boston to Portland, Maine. From there they went to Halifax, Nova Scotia, and took a boat for England.

Parker, in an open letter to President Fillmore, told of the marriage and the couple's escape from the power of the Fugitive Slave Law.

Ellen and William Craft had fled from the land to which two centuries earlier English men and women had come to find freedom. On the island from which these same men and women had fled for lack of freedom, two Negro fugitives from American slavery found for themselves and their children refuge, education, and freedom.

A
MILITANT
MINISTER

THEODORE PARKER

"**K**idnappers in town! They're after William and Ellen Craft," an abolitionist friend gasped, as he hurried into Theodore Parker's third-floor study on a crisp October afternoon in 1850.

"Here, in Boston?" Parker questioned. "But I have advised all fugitive slaves to stay here in Boston. I told them that I had not the smallest fear that one of them would be taken back into bondage. We must act fast!"

This cursed Fugitive Slave Law! It allowed slave owners to send agents to any place in the country to seize runaway slaves and take them back to their masters. Abolitionists in Boston, the center of Eastern antislavery action, passed a local act which penalized any person aiding in the enforcement of the Fugitive Slave Law. In October of 1850, only a month after the Fugitive Slave Law was passed,

Theodore Parker and other abolitionist leaders organized the Boston Vigilance Committee to prevent the recapture of fugitive slaves and to help them in their flight to safety.

To protect the Crafts from the slave agents now in Boston, Parker and his friend decided to call an emergency meeting of the Vigilance Committee.

Committee members, white and Negro, congregated in Theodore Parker's home at Number One, Exeter Street, that afternoon. They consulted behind locked doors and drawn blinds.

Everyone was talking.

"The kidnappers, Knight and Hughes, were arrested for slandering William Craft. They accused him of stealing."

"But now they're out on bail! How will we drive them from the city?"

"Who will be the committee's spokesman to scare them away?"

"Parker?" someone suggested.

"No business for a minister!" another answered sharply.

"Gentlemen," Parker interrupted, "this committee can appoint me to no duty I will not perform. First, we must look out for William and Ellen Craft," he directed. "Take William, well armed, to Lewis Hayden's house."

The Negro Lewis Hayden nodded. He lived in a black community on the back side of Beacon Hill.

His home was a well-known depot of the Underground Railroad.

"I'll see," Parker continued, "that Ellen Craft is made safe. Later, we'll attend to the slave catchers."

In the dead of night, Theodore Parker drove Ellen through Boston. The cab swayed over the cobblestones on its way to an abolitionist's home in Brookline. Holding a hatchet ready for use, the minister sat beside Ellen.

A few days later, the Vigilantes, fearing Ellen's hiding place was under surveillance, rushed her back to Boston. Theodore Parker and his wife took her into their home. Now, whenever Mr. Parker sat at his desk, working on his sermon for the next Sunday, a loaded pistol lay beside his writing tablet.

That same week, Parker led Lewis Hayden and other Vigilantes, sixty in all, into the lobby of the United States Hotel.

"Gentlemen, get out of my hotel," the owner commanded, "or I shall send for the police."

"We stay until we see a Mr. Knight and a Mr.

Hughes." Parker pronounced the names with contempt.

"They are my guests. I will not—" Parker and two others stepped toward him. "I will get your men for you," he gave in.

Knight and Hughes came down the stairway lined with Vigilantes and marched into the crowded lobby.

Theodore Parker stepped forward to meet them. "You are not safe another night in this city of Boston! I have already protected you from violence. I will not do so again. For your own safety, leave at once."

"Slave catchers, remember your ride yesterday? The glass in your carriage door was broken! Those were threats to kill you!" the Vigilantes shouted.

"We thought Boston of all cities was one of law and order. You surprise us," Hughes retorted.

"You'd better make yourselves scarce!" One man raised an arm. In his hand he held a dagger.

"We're taking back a couple of slaves! And not leaving until we . . ." Knight backed up and bumped into Hayden, who raised his arm menacingly. "Don't you touch me!" Knight warned him.

That afternoon, however, the two frightened slave agents abandoned their mission and took a train for New York City. They were not seen again in Boston.

It was decided that the Crafts had better be taken north by the Underground Railroad to a ship leaving for England. Before they left, Parker wished to marry them legally.

Since they all belonged to his congregation, Mr. Parker performed the ceremony before some of the Vigilantes: ". . . and I pronounce you man and wife before God and these witnesses assembled here." He picked up a Bible and put it into William's left hand; in William's right hand he placed a sword. "If the worst comes, use the sword to save your wife's liberty or her life. I give you these dissimilar instruments, one for the body, one for the soul at all events."

By nature Theodore Parker was not a militant man. Although he had never approved the enslavement of any human being, he was nearly forty before he became active in the abolition movement.

Born on a farm in Lexington, Massachusetts, in the beginning of the nineteenth century, he loved the countryside with its meadows and hills, its flowers and fruit trees in blossom. In the fall he would go with his father when he took the peach crop to Faneuil Hall Market, in Boston. To Theodore, Boston was the hub of the universe.

During his boyhood, his chief occupations were farming and learning. His father communicated to his son a love of books and scholarly pursuits. When Theodore was about twenty, he walked from Concord to Cambridge to enroll in Harvard.

While studying at Harvard, he worked as an assistant teacher in a private school in Boston for fifteen dollars a month. He taught languages, mathematics, and philosophy for six hours a day. To take care of the work he would have been doing to help his father on the farm, he hired a man at eleven dollars a month. When his father protested at taking Theodore's money, the young man said, "I cannot let you treat me with any preference over my brothers."

After leaving Harvard, young Parker went to Waterville, not far from Boston, to open his own school. Although he described himself as "a raw boy, with clothes made by country tailors, coarse shoes, great hands, red lips, and blue eyes," he managed to win his future wife there, Lydia Cabot. He also made friends with a Unitarian minister, who encouraged him to attend Harvard Divinity School.

During his seminary years, Parker became a theological rebel. The Bible, he said, was inspired by God but written by fallible man, a denial of the divine authorship of the Bible.

The religious establishment, labeling him heretic and infidel, closed pulpits to him; but all kinds of people flocked to the Melodeon, a theater rented for Sundays, to hear this man preach. His independent congregations became too large for the theater, and they had to rent Boston's Music Theater, which seated three thousand.

Yet he was no orator. He read his sermons earnestly, slowly, for the message must be understood.

The poet James Russell Lowell wrote of him:

> *There he stands looking more like a plough-*
> *man than a priest, . . .*
> *You forget the man wholly, you're thankful to*
> *meet*
> *With a preacher who smacks of the field and*
> *the street.*

Mr. Parker preached that the church exists to right the wrongs of the world. He preached not about the sins of Babylon but about the sins of Boston, about merchants who cut wages in the Lowell mills and about politicians who wrote laws forcing fugitive slaves to be returned to their masters.

It was with real regret that Theodore Parker felt he had to turn from scholarship and theology to active social reform. "I was meant for a philosopher but the times call for a stump orator," he once said.

It is possible, too, that his grandfather, Captain John Parker, who had been an officer in the Revolutionary War, also had some influence on him. On the wall of his study, Theodore Parker hung two muskets, one of which his soldier grandfather had carried into the Battle of Lexington.

The passage of the Fugitive Slave Bill threw Parker into the active ranks of the militant abolitionists. He despised Daniel Webster, Massachusetts senator and later secretary of state, for proposing and defending

Engraved portrait of Theodore Parker. The Boston Athenaeum

this bill, which Webster felt would appease the South and save the Union. Parker not only helped organize the Vigilance Committee of Boston but was ready to fight with force, if need be, to save the Crafts or any other black persons from being thrown again into bondage.

On the other side, white Southerners were ready to go to any length to prevent more slaves escaping from Boston to freedom.

A black named Frederic Williams had run away and reached Boston safely. He took the biblical name Shadrach, after the one whom God saved from the fiery furnace in Babylon. Williams had escaped the fiery furnace of slavery, and in Boston was known by his biblical name.

The morning of February 18, 1851, Marshal Riley arrested Shadrach as a fugitive and took him to the

95

courthouse. That same day, Lewis Hayden and a number of his friends from the black community pushed aside the guards and ran into the courtroom where Shadrach sat for trial.

"Shoot them, shoot them!" Marshal Riley screamed as he saw the invaders.

But no one shot.

Twenty to thirty Negroes seized Shadrach and rushed him from the courtroom to a carriage waiting outside. To try to catch the fugitive, Marshal Riley sent telegrams ordering all trains to stop at state lines. But Shadrach and his rescuers went by horseback. They raced their horses across a bridge over the Charles River, to Cambridge, to Lexington, and to Concord, where they stopped for fresh horses. On they went to Leominster and north to Vermont and Canada and freedom.

Theodore Parker, when he heard of the daring rescue, declared, "Shadrach is delivered out of his burning furnace. . . . I think it is the noblest deed done in Boston since the destruction of tea in 1773."

Theodore Parker believed that to break an evil law made by man, like the Fugitive Slave Law, was to live by the higher law of God. He tried to persuade the Boston Ministerial Conference of this truth. He failed and was renounced by most of Boston's clergymen. Hurt but not defeated by this repudiation by his fellow clergymen, Parker continued his resistance to the Fugitive Slave Law.

On April 3, 1852, authorities arrested and took to the Court House a Negro boy, Thomas Sims, from Georgia. To prevent any repetition of the Craft and Shadrach escapes, authorities had five guards watching him and a dozen officers guarding the stairs. The Court House doors had iron chains across them, and all the windows were barred.

The Vigilance Committee sought different ways in which they might obtain Sims's release. The legal aspects were investigated, such as insufficient evidence, false arrest, right to trial by jury. All failed. Meeting at the office of William Lloyd Garrison's journal, *The Liberator*, the committee made more drastic suggestions.

"Attack the Court House, a hundred of us, and rescue him," one offered.

But there were the chains, the bars, and the guards.

"Steal the records of the southern court from the Judge's desk," another proposed.

But the guards and the chains were there.

"Disable the boat *The Acorn*, which is to carry Sims back to Georgia."

But the city and harbor had been barricaded—all to prevent the escape of one black man!

All their plans fell through. Sims remained prisoner. He begged his lawyer for a knife so that "when the slave commissioner declares me a slave again, I can stab myself."

In the early hours of April 13, the officials hoped to

sneak Sims to the ship while Boston slept. A small group of Vigilantes standing outside aroused Parker and others. Pacing the sidewalk, they and a handful of Negroes and other whites watched Sims as he was marched down State Street, past the very spot where the first man fell in the American Revolution. He was Crispus Attucks, a black. They followed Sims and the soldiers surrounding him to Long Wharf.

As Sims stepped onto the boat, a voice called out, "Sims, preach liberty to the slaves." The watchers sang an adaptation of a familiar hymn:

> *From many a Southern river*
> *And field of sugar cane,*
> *They call us to deliver*
> *Their land from slavery's chain.*

Sims, they learned, was publicly whipped when he landed at Savannah. His owner published in a Boston paper a note of thanks to Boston merchants for their "conspicuous" help in Sims's return.

Humiliated and enraged at the outcome of Sims's case, Parker wrote and posted huge placards of caution: "Colored People of Boston, one and all. Keep a sharp lookout for Kidnappers and have Top Eye Open."

Three years later, on May 24, 1854, at an antislavery convention in Boston, Theodore Parker spoke of Boston's three-year freedom from slave kidnappers and of the rescue of three to four hundred slaves. "Slavery is to perish out of America. Democracy is to triumph."

That same evening, Anthony Burns, a fugitive slave, was on State Street when a marshal and some soldiers seized him.

"You're under arrest for robbing a jewelry store!"

"But I never stole—" Burns, obviously frightened, began.

"I said you stole a man's watch, you hear?"

"Yes, sir."

Without resistance, Anthony Burns went to the Court House, up the stairs, and to the jury room.

A white man came in, took off his hat, and with mock courtesy bowed to Burns. He said, "How do you do, Mr. Burns? Why did you run away from me?"

The fugitive started at the voice and looked up into the face of his former master, Captain Suttle. "I fell asleep on board of the vessel where I worked, and before I woke up, she set sail and carried me off."

"Now, Tony," Captain Suttle said, "haven't I always treated you well?"

The fugitive nodded with resignation. "You've always give me twelve and a half cents a year."

Theodore Parker, as appointed pastor to all fugitive slaves, was admitted to the courtroom. He did not glance at Captain Suttle or the officers but went straight to the black man.

"Burns, we will get a defense counsel for you. You know you have the right to a lawyer. I will bring one."

In a dead voice, Burns said, "No, although I thank you, Reverend Parker. But I will have to go back. My master knows me. His agents know me." He shook his head. "No, Reverend Parker, if I must go back, I want to go as easily as I can."

"As you wish, Burns, but it would do no harm to have a defense."

Burns only shook his head, closed his eyes, and sat silent.

"He seemed stupefied with fear," Theodore Parker told the Vigilantes later.

Parker wrote and had placards printed for the Vigilantes' meeting to be held at Faneuil Hall the next evening.

KIDNAPPING AGAIN

A Man Was Stolen Last Night by the Fugitive Slave Bill Commissioner

He Will Have His

MOCK TRIAL

on Saturday, May 27, at 9 O'Clock,

in the Kidnapper's Court

At the Court House in Court Square

SHALL BOSTON STEAL ANOTHER MAN?

Thursday, May 26, 1854

All of Boston was there. No seat was vacant, the aisles were filled, and the galleries and stairways were packed. Outside, people listened at the windows.

Theodore Parker rose and moved to the roster. He began. "Fellow subjects of Virginia—"

"No, no! Take that back!" members of the audience shouted.

"I will take that back when you show me that it is not so. . . . Gentlemen, I love peace, but there is a means and there is an end. Liberty is the end, and sometimes peace is not the means to it. Now I ask you, what are you going to do?"

"Shoot! Shoot!"

Parker excited the crowd as he waited for the prearranged signal he had worked out with fellow abolitionist Thomas Wentworth Higginson and his men from Worcester. But the signal did not come. Suddenly a shout came from the door. "To the Court House! To the Court House!"

Faneuil Hall emptied. Men raced up the street. Parker ran over the uneven cobblestones.

But it was too late. Higginson's men had already attacked, and without the reinforcement of numbers from Faneuil Hall, the soldiers had easily driven them back. And now soldiers marched through the crowded square to the Court House. The crowd sullenly withdrew.

For ten days the commissioner made rulings on Anthony Burns. For ten days the crowds from

Night attack on the Court House, where Anthony Burns was held captive. Illustration by an artist who was an eyewitness, from *Anthony Burns, A History* by Charles Emery Stevens, Boston, 1856.

Worcester, Springfield, Lexington, and Salem milled before the building. For ten days the militia guarded the Court House. Parker pleaded for Burns's right to liberty. The identification was faulty. Captain Suttle had no proof of ownership with him. But Burns had answered to his name when Suttle spoke to him, and he had said he was willing to go back. The judge ruled the claim was just and gave the prisoner to his owner.

Indignant at the judge's ruling, the women of nearby Woburn sent him the traitor's symbol, thirty pieces of silver, the same sum for which Judas betrayed Christ to his killers.

At ten on a June morning, a six-pound cannon,

102

with forty rounds of shot, was rolled in front of the Court House door. Its muzzle pointed at the waiting crowds.

At noon, soldiers cleared the streets. A cordon of men gripping their muskets lined both sides of the street.

At two in the afternoon, companies of soldiers— the New England Guards, the Washington Light Infantry, the Columbian Artillery, the Bay State Artillery, Marines, lancers, cadets—began their walk. They accompanied Anthony Burns, dressed in a new suit of clothes, down State Street, past stores draped in black, between flags at half-staff. From one window there hung a coffin marked LIBERTY. Thousands watched in funereal silence.

Burns commented, "There was lots of folks to see a colored man walk down the street."

At three that sunny June day, the procession reached the wharf. Church bells began tolling. Boston was a city of tolling bells as Anthony Burns set out on his journey back to slavery.

He was the last slave to be returned to the South from Boston. The Vigilance Committee of Boston successfully protected fugitive slaves and helped them escape to safety. The Fugitive Slave Law was ineffective in the city of Boston.

The Reverend Theodore Parker, however, had not heard the last of the Burns case. As he was writing his Thanksgiving sermon, a visitor was shown in.

"This is a very disagreeable business, Mr. Parker," the man said, handing him an arrest warrant.

"I have no doubt of it," Mr. Parker answered. "But on what grounds am I arrested?"

"You are arrested by the grand jury for obstructing the process of the laws of the United States in slave catching."

"We have only placed justice above man-made law," Parker replied. Actually, he rejoiced at the opportunity this would give him to publicize his position.

On the day of the trial, Parker said in court, "I stand now in as important a position as my honored grandfather at the Battle of Lexington." Fearing the results of Parker's defense, the judge dismissed the case. Not to be robbed of his chance, Parker wrote and had published a five-hundred-page "Defense." He had acted under the higher law in a case involving the freedom of the nation, he wrote.

Now Parker turned to aid in the freeing of slaves elsewhere in the nation. When in 1858 Captain John Brown came to Boston for money to carry on his raids, he was invited to Theodore Parker's home, where he talked for an evening with Garrison, Parker, and Wendell Phillips. He told the men of his plan to invade the South and put weapons into the hands of slaves for insurrection. To Garrison's insistence on nonviolence, John Brown replied, "Without the shedding of blood, there is no remission of sins."

John Brown, from a daguerreotype by Handy, regarded by Brown's family to be the best picture of him. Library of Congress

Convinced of the necessity for force, Parker became one of the Secret Six, a group of men who raised money for John Brown's raids. The Reverend Mr. Parker agreed, "The slave has the right to kill those who enslave him. Free men have the right to help the slave gain freedom."

A man's strength can endure only so much. Theodore Parker, scholar, theologian, reformer, active abolitionist, had taxed himself beyond his power. "I am forty-seven by the reckoning of my mother, seventy-four by my own internal account. I am an *old man.*"

On New Year's Day, 1859, he preached in Boston's Music Hall to an overflowing congregation. He was so weak he had to lean on the pulpit. The next Sunday he had not come by eleven. He had never been late before. Men exchanged alarmed glances. Women whispered, "What can have happened?"

At eleven-thirty, half an hour after the service should have begun, a deacon walked up to the pulpit. From a slip of paper, he read: "Well-beloved friends, I shall not speak to you today, for this morning a little after four o'clock I had a slight attack of bleeding from the lungs. . . . I don't know when I shall again look upon your welcome faces . . .

"May we do justly, love mercy, and walk humbly with our God. His blessing will be upon us . . . for his infinite love is forever and forever."

Because of his health, his wife, Lydia, insisted on their traveling to warmer climates. They were in Florence, Italy, when he died a little over a year after he last preached to his "well-beloved friends." He was buried in the Protestant cemetery there.

After the Civil War, when the ex-slave Frederick Douglass visited Florence, he went to Theodore Parker's grave. As he stood there, he said, "This man Theodore Parker had a voice for the slave when nearly all the pulpits of the land were dumb."

BLACK DISCIPLE OF FREEDOM

CHARLOTTE FORTEN

The small black girl crept to the long window and parted the heavy draperies. She glanced back to the door to make sure she had not been observed.

Through the crack, she saw a gang of .recaptured slaves driven along Lombard Street, in Philadelphia. Their chains clanked; their cries of agony filtered into the silence of the high-ceilinged room. She stuck out her tongue and shook her fists at the mobs of hooting whites hard on their heels. Tears trickled down her cheeks.

"Charlotte, what are you doing?" a distressed voice demanded. "I told you never again to watch the slaves. You pity them so much you make yourself sick."

"But, Mr. Edgar," she sobbed to her handsome black tutor, "I heard their screams and I had to see."

This picture was branded on Charlotte Forten's memory. She was never in her life able to be deaf or blind to the agonies and ignominies of her people, slave or free. She shared every injustice done any black; with every Negro she felt the sting of slavery, the indignity of segregation.

Born in 1838 to freedom and wealth, she lived in the Philadelphia home of her grandfather, James Forten. After serving as powder boy on a ship during the Revolution, he was apprenticed to a sailmaker. Twelve years later he became owner of the business. Through his invention of a device which made it possible to handle sails more easily, he made a hundred thousand dollars, a fortune in those days. He became a distinguished leader of the Negro population of Philadelphia. Charlotte belonged to the fourth generation of Fortens, none of whom had ever known the threats of whip or auction block.

But neither freedom nor money, even in the North, could shield a black child from prejudice. Observation and personal experience taught her the limitations in the position allotted to blacks.

"I want to go to school like Tansy," the girl begged her father. "Why won't you let me?"

"Charlotte, you're too young to understand, but some white people think we're different because we have a different-colored skin," Robert Bridges Forten tried to explain to her. "My father, your grandfather, fought for his belief that all of us, black and white, are the same, made by the same God, and should have the same liberty and be protected by the same laws. Do you understand?"

The little girl nodded. "But why can't I go to school?"

"The white people want black children to go to black schools. Separate schools insult us!"

Charlotte continued her lessons with her tutor.

Everywhere she went, the white world drummed into her that her race was inferior. "Step back, I say, to the rear of the carriage." Concerts, lectures, a performance of *Hamlet* were closed to her because she was black. "What do you want with Shakespeare?" she was told. At an ice cream parlor, "You can't eat here!" In a department store, not a word from the saleslady, only a long stare before the clerk flounced away.

Charlotte's home life taught her far different lessons about her race. Very young when her mother died, she spent weeks at a time with her Aunt Harriet, who had married Robert Purvis. He raised champion livestock and lived in the manner of the gentry in Byberry, an affluent estate outside Philadelphia. More important, he and his wife made Byberry a center for distinguished abolitionists, white and black, and their antislavery activities. Here Charlotte absorbed discussions of fugitive slave laws, abolitionist conventions, and racial injustices. In protective darkness, she saw fugitive slaves spirited out of the house on their way to the Underground Railroad.

Brought up on such doctrines, how could the white man's attitude of black inferiority be anything but unacceptable to her?

A dedicated disciple of the religion of racial equality, Charlotte set out to prove that the black was as intelligent as the white. She felt compelled to excel in her every pursuit, and she expected every other black to achieve excellence as well. One birthday she asked herself, "Have I improved as much as I should?"

A lonely child, she began keeping a journal at an early age. Her father, realizing Charlotte's need of companions her own age, sent her to Salem, Massachusetts, where the schools were integrated.

Living there with the Remond family, Charlotte was again among ardent abolitionists. When she first arrived, excitement was running high over the capture of the fugitive slave, Anthony Burns, in the Boston streets. The Remonds took her to see him surrounded by soldiers with fixed bayonets. All to prevent one man's regaining his rightful freedom! She despised the soldiers guarding his prison while he was on trial. "They made my blood boil. I have only contempt for such cowardice and servility."

Such episodes haunted her. They shadowed her every happiness.

One June morning she looked happily out her window for the bird whose song she was hearing. She spotted a robin in a nearby apple tree. In her journal she said, "His song was sweeter to me than the clearer tones of the canary birds in their cages, for they are captives, while he is free! I would not keep even a bird in bondage."

Her studies were her chief concern in Salem. At Higginson Grammar School, she made fast friends with the principal, Mary Shepard. She filled her journal with praises of "dear Miss Shepard." She noted a Saturday walk in the woods. "We talked of many things and I feel blessed and happy as I always do in the society of my beloved teacher."

A shy girl, Charlotte was fearful of showing her emotions, perhaps because of past rebuffs. Once before vacation, when Miss Shepard thanked her for helping and gave her a friendly pat, Charlotte was distressed at her own instinctive withdrawal. "She must think me cold. Yet when I feel most, I say least. I hate to part even a few weeks from her."

With her classmates, she felt insecure. After one vacation, she told her journal, "Most of them greeted me cordially and were it not for the thought that *will* intrude, of the want of *entire sympathy* even in those I know and like best, I should greatly enjoy their society."

One day when she was walking on Salem's Federal Street, she met two classmates who had always seemed friendly to her in school. She smiled and greeted them. The two barely nodded to her and continued their conversation.

"Oh, it is hard to go through life . . . fearing with too good reason to love and trust hardly anyone whose skin is white—however lovable, attractive, congenial in seeming."

These slights deepened her resentment into bitterness toward her native land, "where I am hated and oppressed because God has given me a dark skin." She scorned the Fourth of July celebrations of liberty as hypocrisy. Relics of the American Revolution in Philadelphia's Independence Hall were to her "a mockery, . . . here where there breathes not a freeman, black or white." Her resentment nearly made her renounce God and her religion. "How *can* I be a Christian when so many in common with myself, for no crime, suffer cruelty, so unjustly?"

Scholastically, Charlotte proved herself the equal of her fellow students. To test her intellectual capacity, she read within the year over one hundred books beyond the required reading and independently studied French and Latin.

A member of the 1855 February graduating class, Charlotte anonymously submitted a farewell poem. The words were set to music. No one, not even the principal, knew the author. ·

"Will the boy or girl who wrote this farewell song

please rise," Miss Shepard requested after the singing. "And come forward."

No one rose.

"Author! Author!"

Hesitantly, Charlotte Forten, the only Negro in the class, stood and with embarrassment walked down the aisle to the platform.

Astonished, the aristocratic Salem audience watched the dark, slight girl with her finely sculptured features mount the steps and join Miss Shepard on the stage. Their silence burst into loud and long applause.

Charlotte graduated with honors from Salem Normal School, which had accepted her without question of color. She was appointed to a Salem public school, and she became the first Negro to teach whites in Massachusetts.

During her teaching years in Salem, she worked hard in the classroom while she continued her other two interests, abolition and scholarship. She attended many antislavery meetings as well as lectures by Ralph Waldo Emerson and James Russell Lowell.

Never physically strong, she often told her journal of headaches and of a feeling of illness. After a trip to Cambridge to see Longfellow's home, she was so weary she felt it necessary to sleep all day. "Dear Mary Shepard brought me flowers," she wrote. Then, doctors discovered Charlotte had lung fever. Teach-

Charlotte Forten. Association for the Study of Negro Life and History

ing, abolition work, and study proved too much for her, and for three years she had to alternate teaching in Salem with rests in Byberry.

To her sorrow, ill health finally forced her to resign from her teaching position altogether. The Salem *Register* regretted her leaving: "Miss Forten is a young lady of color. . . . We are happy to record this instance of the success of the lady as a teacher in our public school."

For the next four years she recuperated in Philadelphia, "a city that is most hateful," she wrote. Intermittently she was well enough to teach in her aunt's school and to enter antislavery activities. At the same time, she was writing some poetry. She also wrote sketches called "Glimpses of New England," several of which were published.

Her rest made her well enough in 1862 to jump into the Union's exciting experiment in South Carolina. Early in the Civil War (1861), the North had captured Port Royal and Sea Island off Charleston Harbor. Here, there were some ten thousand slaves who were left behind when their masters fled before the Union forces. Lincoln's government decided to send Northerners to teach the abandoned slaves and also to train the men to fight.

These black people, because of generations of slavery and geographic isolation, were the least educated and assimilated of all Southern slaves. The occupying Union army could hardly understand their speech. With no government funds available, Northern benevolent societies raised money for the cause. By March, fifty-three men and women, all white, were teaching these blacks.

Now Charlotte had her chance to demonstrate her life-long thesis, the black man's capacity to learn. As a Negro, she had difficulty being accepted for a teaching position, but finally left for the South under the auspices of the Philadelphia Port Royal Society.

The night of her arrival in South Carolina, a black crew rowed her from the mainland to St. Helena's Island, her destination. She felt very far away from

115

home. But the men's singing in rhythm with the oars helped reassure her.

> *Jesus make de blind to see*
> *Jesus make de deaf to hear*
> *Jesus make de cripple walk*
> *Walk in, dear Jesus.*

Once on the island, a driver took her through rows of trees ghosted by hanging moss, all the time singing, "John Brown body lie a moldin' in de groun'."

She was thankful to reach Oaklands, an abandoned and dilapidated planter's home she was to share with two other teachers. Tense from excitement, she could

An 1866 engraving of a meeting of freedmen on St. Helena's Island, South Carolina. The Schomburg Collection, New York City

not sleep. With only blankets for a mattress, she tossed and turned on the "bones of the bed."

In the morning the cackling of chickens and the cheerful voices of men, women, and children greeted her. Jumping out of bed, she hurried to the window, to see women with bright headkerchiefs crossing the yard. Children were playing and tumbling among the women. "Out of de way—don' trip me."

Every face was happy, Charlotte thought and laughed to herself. And they should be, for they were free! So long downtrodden, now forever free! Thank God. She breathed deeply the heady scent of freedom and of roses in blossom.

Later that morning, she walked the mile from Oaklands to the Baptist church, where on weekdays school was held. The sandy road went through pines and live oaks draped with hanging moss and tangles of mistletoe.

Charlotte Forten found teaching here much more rewarding than in the North. Everyone here, children and adults, longed to learn. In summer, the older boys and girls worked in the hot fields from dawn until ten or eleven in the morning. But afterwards they came eagerly to school. A young woman with a baby in her arms never missed a day. A grandmother, all of sixty, was there every day and sat with the little ones for lessons. Little children were happy to hold a book in their hands. "I like to have my scholars about me and see the smiles of greeting break over their dusky faces," she wrote in her journal.

Conditions, however, were not easy. With as many as a hundred and forty in one room, she had to strain her voice to be heard. Many were too small to learn the alphabet. But without the babies, the older brothers and sisters could not have come. Unaccustomed to study, the older ones had a very brief attention span.

Charlotte insisted her pupils learn about Negro as well as white heroes in history; about blacks who fought in the American Revolution; about Negroes like her uncle Robert Purvis, who helped fugitive slaves on their way to Canada; about Toussaint, the Negro liberator of Haiti; about John Brown of Harper's Ferry, the black man's white friend.

Evenings, the children came to Oaklands for "shouts," a strange ceremony. They formed a ring and moved around in a shuffling dance. Four or five musicians stood apart, clapping their hands, stamping their feet, rocking their bodies back and forth, and led in singing hymns.

> *Go down in de lonesome valley*
> *To meet my Jesus dere*

Three- and four-year-olds joined in the "shouting" as vigorously as the older ones. Little Amaretta, of whom Charlotte was very fond, begged to "shout" her favorites, "What make ole Satan follow me?" and

"Christ build de church widout no hammer and no nail."

On her first Christmas morning on St. Helena's, Charlotte heard a knocking at her window. "Merry Christmas," she sang out. She joined the boys and girls who had come to fetch her. They hurried to the church, which they had decorated with holly, pine, mistletoe, and hanging moss. She smiled into their faces, glistening now with a happiness they had never known before.

"Amaretta, Prince, Tom, Angie." She called out the names, as she took gifts from the huge box from Philadelphia. There was a present for each one— bright cloth for a dress, shirt material, a book, alphabet blocks, picture cards.

"Thank you, Ma'am," even the youngest remembered.

She led them in the Christmas song her friend Mr. John Greenleaf Whittier had written especially for Charlotte's pupils.

"And this evening," she told them, "come to Oaklands for 'shouts.' "

Late that night, after the "shouters" had left, Charlotte observed, "This is the happiest Christmas they've ever had. Or that I've ever had," she added to herself.

She found the years at St. Helena's fulfilling in other ways also.

In the evenings, some adults who worked all day

came to her for instruction. There was Harry, a plantation foreman, of whom she wrote: "I never saw anyone more determined to learn." Painstakingly she taught him how to hold a pen and form letters.

She liked to hear him tell "how Massa run when he hear de first gun."

"Why didn't you go with him, Harry?"

"Massa try to git me. Say de Yankees'd shoot me or sen' me to Cuba. But I decide I as good as dead wid Massa. Couldn' be worse off here—even wid de Yankees. An' somehow hear de Yankees our frien's."

Charlotte often went to the Corner, a settlement of Negro homes. While cutting out a dress for Venus, an old woman there, she asked, "Has the past year been happy for you, Venus?"

"Oh, yes, Missus. Nobody to whip me nor dribe, an' plenty to eat. Nebber had such a happy year in life before."

Sometimes she helped in the settlement store and chatted with different customers. "Susie, do some of you sometimes wish you had your old masters back?"

"No, no Missus, dey treat we too bad. Dey take ebery one of my chillun away from me. Only fool wan massa back!"

The Negro regiment, trained to fight with the Union troops, made Charlotte especially proud. It fought bravely even though the attack on Charleston was unsuccessful. The blacks proved they could stand up in battle as courageously as the whites. For there

120

were many whites in the Union government and army who did not believe this. With pride Charlotte went to the hospital to nurse the wounded black men.

All this time she was recording in her journal her impressions of the events and people on St. Helena's. Some of these she sent to Whittier, through whom they were published in the *Atlantic Monthly* under the title, "Life on the Sea Islands."

The life here gave Charlotte new self-confidence. Perhaps for the first time, she saw other people as neither white nor black but as human beings. She and two white men, an army doctor who had treated her

Sea Islanders in Union uniform outside former slave quarters in 1862. Photograph by H. P. Moore. New York Historical Society, New York City

in Massachusetts and a Rhode Island educator, enjoyed each other's company.

Dr. Rogers came to dine. Afterwards they rode through the woods. When assigned to Florida for a short time, he sent her a gift, "a very pretty light rocking chair," she described it. Together they read Emerson aloud.

For lack of a confidante, she wrote in her journal to an imaginary "Chère Amie" of the friendship: "It is pleasant to know he cares so much for me, even though I *know* he thinks far better of me than I deserve."

She also went riding with Mr. Thorpe, the teacher. "How strange and wild it seemed riding through the woods—often in such darkness we c'ld see nothing— how strange and wild! I like it."

Much as Charlotte enjoyed Dr. Rogers and Mr. Thorpe, she could not completely forget the barrier. She told "Chère Amie," "I am black and he [Mr. Thorpe] is white. . . . Report says that he more than likes me. But I *know* it is not so. . . . Although he is very good and liberal, he is still an American, and w'ld, of course, never be so insane as to love one of the proscribed race."

The intensity of her work, the days and evenings with children and adults, the hard physical conditions brought a return of her headaches and the threat of another bout with lung fever. With stark resignation, she wrote in her journal, "It is necessary for my health; therefore, it is wise to go north."

After some four or five months of resting in the Pennsylvania mountains, she went back to her mission on St. Helena's Island and stayed there until the end of the Civil War.

The twelve years after the Civil War were quiet for Charlotte Forten. She lived in Philadelphia with her writing and her studies. The *Atlantic Monthly* published two more of her articles on the Fort Royal experiment.

They were quiet but significant years, for during that time she met the Grimké sisters' nephew Francis Grimké. With him she again entered the mainstream of the black struggle for equality.

They were naturally drawn to each other. His background fired her sympathy. He was the illegitimate son of Henry Grimké, a prominent citizen of Charleston, and a black slave woman.

"My father, before his death, made my white half-brother promise to set me free," Francis told Charlotte. "But instead of freeing me, he threatened to sell me. So at ten I ran away."

"Oh, no," she barely breathed. "But how . . . ?"

"After the war, I managed to enter Lincoln University, and my father's sister, Angelina Grimké, an abolitionist, saw my name in the paper. She acknowledged me as her nephew and has made it possible for me to go to Princeton Theological Seminary."

Their admiration for one another soon turned into love. A few months before his graduation from theological seminary, they were married.

With the same urge to fight social injustices and with similar literary tastes, they made a happy pair. The death of their only child and her need to fight constantly against recurrent illness cast the only shadows on their personal happiness.

In Washington, D.C., where Francis was pastor of a church for many years, Charlotte and he crusaded against the system which demeaned and penalized men and women for being black.

For another generation, if not for themselves, Charlotte Forten and Francis Grimké envisioned a new earth. She wrote of a time "when prejudice shall vanish before the glorious light of Liberty and Truth; when the rights of every colored man shall everywhere be acknowledged and respected, and he shall be treated as Man and Brother."

COMMANDED BY GOD

SARAH DICKEY

A bullet glanced by her cheek and lodged in the pulpit behind her. It had whizzed through the door, left open to let the night air cool the stuffy church.

Thirty persons rose as one and gasped, "Miss Dickey!" Sarah Dickey barely paused before continuing with her evening class of black men and women.

Every night after supper, they hurried to the Baptist church, the only one in Clinton, Mississippi, which would allow its building to be used for teaching blacks. Here, in 1871, Miss Dickey began teaching the new freedmen to read, write, and work with figures.

The shot had not surprised her. A week before, she had received a letter with a printed message: "Go North where you came from. If you're still here after ten days, you will walk to school through bullets and brickbats. You will rest at night under the same treatment."

The insults hurled at her since she had come to Clinton were harder to bear than fear of physical violence. She had come for the Freedmen's Bureau to open a "free school." Clinton citizens, like all white citizens of the state, were outraged at the idea and expense of giving education to their former slaves.

Everywhere, Sarah Dickey met hostility.

"No, I've no room to let," a white housemistress flung at Sarah. "And if I did, I'd not let it to you! You Yankees meddle too much! No, I've no room for such as you!"

Finally, Senator Caldwell, one of the newly elected blacks in the Reconstruction State Legislature, offered her room and board with his family. For three years Miss Dickey was a member of his household. Such disloyalty to her own race made Clinton hate her more.

At church, a Southern lady, seeing Miss Dickey enter the pew, departed as if from a leper. On the street women pulled their skirts aside so as not to have them contaminated by touching Sarah's. Boys hooted at her. Carrying a tightly rolled cotton umbrella, she threatened to break it over their heads.

The morning after the bullet incident, a prominent Clinton resident warned her. "Miss Dickey, for your own welfare, be on your way home."

"Sir, I have been called to the South to do God's will. Only death will force me to leave!"

And for thirty years, until her death, Sarah Dickey did teach in Clinton. She had responded to the call to educate Negroes, teach them to become independent, self-respecting citizens.

Sarah Dickey was born in 1838. From her own hard experience, she knew the vital importance of education. At thirteen she could neither read nor write.

When she was eight, her mother died. Her father parceled out his eight children to relatives in southwestern Ohio. For five years Sarah was with an aunt who promised the girl would have schooling in return for helping with the housework. When her father came to see his daughter, he found she had been an excellent helper but had not once been inside a school.

Although she could not read a book, Sarah had an inner drive to learn. "Father, please, a place where I can go to school. I'll work, but school."

Her father tried again and found a widow on a farm. "My daughter's a good worker. And she wants to go to school. That's understood?"

For nearly four weeks Sarah attended classes, but the farm was too demanding. Morning and afternoon, winter and summer, she drove the cows a mile to pasture and back. She split and brought in wood to feed the fire. Meals had to be prepared, dishes washed, clothes ironed. She became so sickly the widow had no further use for her.

Her father placed her this time with a cousin. "And remember, Sarah's to go to school."

Sarah went for two winters—ten to fifteen days a winter.

This taste of learning whetted her appetite for more, and she resolved to become a teacher.

"But you're sixteen! You can barely read and write. You'll be in the same grade as the children."

"You're not bright enough to be a teacher. Don't you know that?"

Her family pelted her with such slurs, and all had the same question. "Where'll you get the money?"

Not to be deflected from her purpose, she found a neighbor who let her earn her room and board and go to school. For three years, Sarah was up at four in the morning and did the chores. After school she washed, helped with the supper, and did the dishes. Until ten she ironed and mended clothes. After ten she was free to do her own lessons.

Resolutely, Sarah met the hard demands and at nineteen graduated from secondary school with a teacher's certificate.

By fall she had a teaching position nine miles from where she was living. An eighteen-mile walk a day! And it was a difficult school.

"We have some big boys; they're hard. They've driven more than one teacher off," the president of the school committee warned her as he sized up the young woman applicant. "Think you can handle them?"

"I can try."

She got the position and won over the school.

After that, schools sought Sarah. But she felt the need of further education and alternated her teaching with study.

On her twentieth birthday, she joined the Church of the United Brethren in Christ. Though without formal religious training, she had always sensed a higher companion in her lonely existence. In her church she found human and spiritual fellowship. It had a life-long influence on her. For the last eight years of her life she was an ordained clergyman of her church.

Although she lived in Ohio, which like many other northern states had by 1830 outlawed slavery by legislative, judicial or constitutional action, most people still sympathized with the southern slave owners. She herself had long despised slavery, especially its cruel deprivation of education to children. She believed herself called to teach them.

The Mission Board of the United Brethren gave Sarah Dickey the opportunity she sought. It sent her to Vicksburg, Mississippi, in December, 1863, two years after the beginning of the Civil War. She found a ravaged city where thirty thousand people had taken refuge.

She and two other teachers moved into a former Union army hospital where some soldiers were still quartered. It was dirty; the floors were bloodstained.

The first night there, Sarah saw flames shooting out of a hole in the corner chimney of her second-floor room. Seizing a bucket of water she had just dragged up the stairs, she doused the fire.

"Hey! Where's that water coming from? Soaking the few sticks we managed to find! Our fire's out!" shouted the cold and indignant soldiers from below.

The school numbered around three hundred Negro pupils. When it started, not more than a dozen could read and only one could write. By the end of the next year, even with irregular attendance, some one hundred could read the New Testament, and fifty were good in penmanship, geography, and arithmetic. All had improved in self-confidence and had become more aware of personal health and hygiene.

In addition to teaching, Miss Dickey helped blacks with marital relations. As slaves they had not been allowed legal marriage; now they longed for its dignity. Sarah made out certificates for more than three thousand marriages. After counseling with the couples, she contacted the Union chaplain for mass ceremonies.

For nineteen months, until Lee's surrender at Appomattox, she worked in Vicksburg. With the Freedmen's Bureau taking over education, the United Brethren mission closed, and Sarah returned

This engraving of a primary school for freedmen in Vicksburg, Mississippi, appeared in Harper's Weekly, *June 23, 1866.* Library of Congress

to the North. She was now convinced she must have higher education to accomplish her goal for these black people she had come to love.

Back in Ohio, she was determined to go on to college. Her sister had much admired a teacher from Mount Holyoke with whom she had studied. Once she said to Sarah, "If only you could go to Mount Holyoke Seminary!" But it was too far away. Sarah applied at Earlham, a Quaker college in Richmond, Indiana, but was refused entrance. As she questioned what to do, she heard an inner voice saying to her,

"Go to Mount Holyoke Seminary." It was miles and miles away, and she had no money.

Undaunted, she borrowed some money from her church and within two weeks set out for South Hadley, Massachusetts. Her train ticket took her only as far as Albany, New York. In her hurry she forgot to take food for the long trip. Her mouth watered as fellow passengers enjoyed sandwiches and chicken drumsticks. While they ate, she studied the passing landscape. During the thirty-four-hour journey from Ohio to Albany, Sarah went without food.

In Albany she approached the ticket agent. "How do I get to South Hadley?"

"Take the train to Springfield. There's a ferry there. Takes you across the Connecticut River and then—"

"As far as that! But I've no money for the ticket or the ferry."

"No money! You've no business going on a journey without plenty of cash," the agent berated her. "You going to your family in South Hadley?"

"No. To Mount Holyoke Seminary."

"Teach there?"

"No, a student."

The agent stared at Sarah, obviously too old to be going to school. But she looked honest and bright.

"I tell you, Miss, you leave your trunk here as collateral, and I'll advance enough for your fare." To himself he added, "Fool that I am!"

Sarah Dickey, twenty-nine years old, arrived at Mount Holyoke with exactly thirty-four cents in her purse. She was late for the fall term. The seminary had never heard of her. She had no money for the $125.00 annual tuition. She was in debt to her church. She owed her fare to the ticket agent in Albany.

Mount Holyoke gave her entrance tests, and she passed easily; members of the faculty chipped in the money to redeem her trunk; a pupil's dropping out gave her a job so she could pay her way; a man had left sixty dollars for some needy student. Almost miraculously, she became a member of the class of 1869. Of the original hundred in the class, only thirty-eight graduated, Sarah Dickey among them.

During her time at the seminary, prompted by her inner voice, she resolved to found a southern Mount Holyoke for Negro girls. But after her graduation, exhausted by her strenuous physical and scholastic work, burdened with debts, she returned to her sister in Ohio. To most, achievement of her goal would have seemed impossible. But her faith assured her a way would open, even as Mount Holyoke had.

The way came through the American Missionary Association, which sent her to work in Raymond, Mississippi. After a short stay, the Freedmen's Bureau asked her to open the "free school" in Clinton.

By the end of three years in Clinton, Sarah Dickey had paid her personal debts. She did not hesitate to borrow again for the school she intended to establish for Negro girls. There was a brick house on the outskirts of Clinton. Before the war it had been a white girls' school. Large, with white columns and a big assembly room, it was ideal.

By paying ten dollars down and on payment of the first three thousand dollars, Sarah was to acquire the property. The white owners were confident they would recover it when the second three-thousand-dollar payment came due. This Yankee could never raise the sum! Times were bad. A local bank had closed its doors. Businesses were failing. But the resolute woman went to other women, mostly black, and persuaded them of the benefits of such a school to their children. Through barbecues, suppers, and other money-raising events, the first thousand dollars was raised.

Then Miss Dickey headed north on the first of her many money-raising expeditions. She went to her Mount Holyoke classmates and to mission boards. She got letters of introduction to wealthy people. In Cincinnati she received a two-hundred-dollar gift for furniture for Mount Hermon. She had named her new school after the mountain in Palestine. By summer she had the three thousand dollars necessary to take possession and open the school in September.

The astonished house owners were not ready to leave, but they allowed Sarah to move in, if she would postpone the school's opening.

The postponement proved to be a blessing. With

134

elections coming, Senator Caldwell organized a Republican rally. Although he had warned Negroes not to bring liquor or guns, two white men brought in liquor and resisted black policemen who tried to stop them. The white men were both killed in the ensuing fight.

Four days of horror followed. Governor Ames sent Negro troops, who marched through Clinton beating drums. The whites were further enraged at this display by their former slaves. Senator Caldwell, tricked into the basement of a business building, was shot in the back. Lying there wounded, he said, "Gentlemen, don't shoot anymore. I am dying and I want to see my wife." As they continued to shoot, he gasped, "All right. Fire away and see how a brave man can die."

Had Mount Hermon been open with its Negro pupils, it would surely have been destroyed in the orgy of white revenge. With a white family still living there, the mobs left it unharmed.

Mount Hermon opened later that year with Sarah Dickey as headmistress and a board of trustees that was half black and half white. Both groups agreed to serve but each refused to meet with the other. To the black trustees, Miss Dickey sent notes asking them to meet her at the school at two o'clock the following Tuesday. To the white trustees, she sent notes asking them to meet her at the same place and time. Both groups came. Amused at her clever manipulation, they held board meetings together after that. Within five years the school and its head had won deep black devotion and some white acclaim.

The work which Sarah Dickey did alone was almost incredible. She administered and found funds to support the school. She directed the farming of the land and herself canned much of the produce for the school's food.

Climbing up and down ladders, she supervised the upkeep of and additions to the buildings. A former pupil returned to see her when she was old and ill. He went to her room, expecting to find her in bed, but discovered her on the third floor personally directing workmen.

When the town closed the "freedmen's school"—no need for two schools for "niggers"—she took in as day pupils all the black boys and girls of Clinton.

Beyond the usual subject matter, she taught attitudes toward life.

Since the blacks had no clocks in their cabins, the children often came to school very early or very late. To instill a sense of time and promptness, she acquired a sturdy brass bell. Mornings, its clapper called the pupils to school. Afternoons, mothers listened for its clapper to tell them to expect their children home. To prevent loitering, Miss Dickey sometimes rode behind them. Mounted on her horse, she was quite a figure. A Negro said of her, "She drove a span of horses like a man."

She trained many black girls as teachers. Neighboring schools were eager to hire graduates of the teacher-training course. Many became assistants in Mount Hermon.

As at Mount Holyoke, every girl did some daily household task with emphasis on neatness and cleanliness. A course in sewing stressed independence. Each girl made her own commencement suit and mortarboard. The humanities were learned through music and literature. The Bible was studied and loved.

Miss Dickey's talks at the Sunday evening services and at morning chapels made deep impressions on the pupils. One grown woman recalled Miss Dickey as a preacher: "An extra fine voice, clear for carrying. It seemed to ring. You remembered what she said. She talked a lot about starting right where you were. Forget past mistakes and bad things. Put all you've got into today and then, when it comes, into tomorrow." Another said of her, "You always understood her when she talked. She took time to tell you good. She was patient but firm."

When there was good reason, Miss Dickey did not hesitate to punish, even using the whip before she prayed with the guilty one. "But she always played fair," a former pupil commented.

She developed her pupils' pride in their race and protected them from indignities.

One day she sent two girls for the mail. On the

narrow sidewalk, two boards wide, they met the finely dressed wife of the white postmaster. Their skirts brushed against hers.

"How dare you? Get off the sidewalk!" The lady hastened into the post office and reported the incident to her husband.

The postmaster rushed out, ran to a nearby harness shop, seized a whip, and ran at the girls. Terrified, they stood stock still. There on the Clinton street, the postmaster publicly whipped them. After that, Miss Dickey sent them on horseback for the mail. She also consulted a white lawyer who had worked with her. Within two months, there was a new postmaster.

She never forgot her own homeless childhood and remembered the home Mount Holyoke had been to her. She decided that Mount Hermon should shelter deserted or fatherless children and took in many whose fathers had died. At that time, if a black child had a white father who died, the child was left homeless, since to leave anything to a black mistress or to black children was illegal. Mount Hermon was home to Willette Campbell, who graduated from the teacher-training course, taught in the school and was married from there. Miss Dickey sent Eddie Messenger, a promising pupil, to Tougaloo Univeristy, in Mississippi. She also became foster mother to Mary Caldwell after Senator Caldwell's death.

Miss Dickey wasn't always successful with her wards. One ran away after a whipping and was never

Sarah A. Dickey. This portrait hangs in Sarah A. Dickey Memorial Hospital at Tougaloo College, Tougaloo, Mississippi.

heard from; another had to be sent back to Mobile for corrupting the others. But to the majority, Miss Dickey was teacher, guardian, and mother.

She looked out for the old as well as for the young. Knowing there was no place for the old and sick in the crowded Negro shacks, she had cabins built on the campus for women like Granny Sukey.

As their watchdog in business dealings with whites, Miss Dickey accompanied Negroes when they went to get their payment for the year's cotton. She guarded them against unfair loan and interest practices, which were very common.

Seeing freedmen still living in miserable plantation huts, she conceived an idea of independent housing for them. She called them together to present her plan.

"Between the village and Mount Hermon, 120 acres of land are available."

Her listeners knew about the unused land, but what had it to do with them? Still, Miss Dickey never fooled them. They hung on her next words.

"I can borrow money."

They knew she could borrow. One time she had gone to the bank to borrow five hundred dollars for the school. "How long will it take to arrange the loan?" she had asked the banker.

"I'll give it to you right now, Miss Sarah."

Their minds and ears sharpened. "I will buy the land, have it surveyed, and sell the lots to you at twenty dollars an acre. Without interest."

Each family envisioned its own home standing on its own acre plot, flowers blooming around the stoop with children playing in the yard.

True to her constant insistence on black independence, Miss Sarah added, "But you must find work to pay for the land and build your own homes."

The blacks decided to buy the first lot for a community church, the Holy Ghost Baptist Church. It stood there and was used until 1964, when it and thirty-seven other Mississippi black churches were burned to the ground in the backlash against black voter registration.

The housing project, named Dickeyville, became a law-abiding, self-respecting community, which still exists today.

Age and chronic rheumatism made Miss Dickey's annual fund-raising excursions to the North increasingly difficult. But she was resolute, even if unsuccessful, in trying to secure a permanent endowment for Mount Hermon. She persisted in her efforts until at sixty-six she developed fatal pneumonia.

The Negroes grieved when she died. They loved this woman who had lived and worked with them and saw them as her brothers. Multitudes of black and some white friends packed the school chapel, where a black clergyman conducted the funeral services. She was buried in a stand of pine trees on the campus at Mount Hermon. Granny Sukey and two orphan girls whom Miss Sarah had befriended lie beside her.

The *Hinds County Gazettte*, which had violently opposed education for blacks, paid final tribute to her: "She was a woman of strong character, devoted to her work among the blacks and did not seem to care if she was socially ostracized. She maintained that she was commanded by God to come South and labor in the field that she occupied, and no power on earth could change her."

Fortunately she never knew that in spite of loyal black efforts to buy the school, it was forced to close in 1924, twenty years after her death, and the buildings were set on fire by delinquent boys.

But Sarah Dickey's faith had never faltered. She believed the work to which God had called her would continue. Just before her death, with firm conviction, she said, "All is well. All is done. Good-bye. Let the work go on as usual."

PROPHET OF FREEDOM

ELIJAH LOVEJOY

"Abolitionist!"

"You promised not to print antislavery articles! Liar!"

"We'll get you and your press!"

A clod of dirt, hard as rock, hit the Reverend Elijah Lovejoy's shoulder.

He was hurrying home from the apothecary shop with some medicine for his wife, who was very ill.

The men who had threatened him now linked arms and blocked his path.

The quarter moon shone clear through the gathering darkness of this late August evening in 1837.

The young clergyman looked at his obstructors. "Gentlemen, why have you stopped me?" he asked.

"Alton, Illinois, wants no slave lover!"

"Trying to incite slaves to rise against their God-given masters!"

142

"Rail him!" One of the men swung a heavy club as if he were going to hit Lovejoy.

"Tar and feather him!" they shouted. "We've a kettle of tar with a fire laid under it. And pillows full of feathers!"

"You had better let me go home." Lovejoy tried to reason with the dozen men. "You have no right to detain me. I have never injured you."

"Tar and feather him!" they repeated.

"All right. I am in your hands, and you must do with me whatever you please. I have but one request," Lovejoy asked calmly. "My wife is dangerously ill. Will you take this medicine to her?" He held out a small package. "And please give it to her without alarming her."

All were silent. No one offered to take the medicine. Then one man put out his hand.

"Thank you." To the others Lovejoy said, "I am in the hands of God and am ready to go with you."

No one spoke until a man with a deep Southern drawl said, "Boys, I can't lay my hands upon a man as brave as this man is." He walked away and the rest followed him.

They let the Reverend Elijah Lovejoy go home to his sick wife, but they raided his office and, for the second time since he had come to Alton, Illinois, destroyed his new printing press, and dropped the pieces into the Mississippi.

Until four years before this incident, this young

man's life had not been unusual. Born in a small Maine town on the bank of the Kennebec River, Elijah Lovejoy had plowed the land, fished and swum in the lakes and river, gone on parish calls with his father, a Congregational minister. After receiving his bachelor's degree from Waterville College (now Colby College), he taught for a year in Maine. Like other young men of the early 1800s, he felt the urge to go west. With almost no money—he had eighty cents when he reached Boston—he worked his way west as far as Saint Louis, Missouri.

Here he taught, did some reporting for the Saint Louis *Times*, and felt the urge to become a clergyman like his father. In less than fifteen months, Elijah Lovejoy had completed the three-year course at Princeton Theological Seminary in New Jersey. He was offered the position of editor of a Presbyterian weekly paper, the Saint Louis *Observer*. Rather than seek a pulpit in the East as he had planned, he decided to go back to Saint Louis.

On November 12, 1833, Elijah Lovejoy returned to Missouri. He was thirty-one years old. The Missouri to which he came was a strong proslavery state. One of the most despised labels a man could have was abolitionist, advocate of the immediate freeing of slaves. Local newspapers condemned all antislavery discussion or reports on antislavery activities by leaders like William Lloyd Garrison back in the East.

The *Observer* had vehemently denounced liquor

Elijah P. Lovejoy

and the pomp and vanity of the world. On other social questions of the day, of which slavery was the foremost, its position had been moderate. This did not trouble the new editor. Although he advocated the gradual freeing of slaves, he was not an abolitionist. "Slavery could not be abolished without doing untold damage to both masters and slaves," he wrote in his paper.

By the fall of 1835, events in Saint Louis led to drastic changes in his point of view.

The Saint Louis *Commercial Bulletin*, a daily paper, declared Elijah Lovejoy guilty of sending out copies of the abolitionist journal *The Emancipator*. While packing some Bibles in a box one day, he stuffed some newspapers around them to prevent the books from shifting. Inadvertently, he had grabbed some *Emancipators* lying in his office. Missourians labeled him an abolitionist in spite of his statement: "I have never knowingly sent any abolition publication to a single individual in Missouri or elsewhere." But along with this denial he declared, "Yet I have the right to send a thousand if I choose regardless of any mob decree."

The citizens of Saint Louis formed a Committee of Vigilance to stop all antislavery talk and especially to silence Lovejoy and his *Observer,* where he had proclaimed slavery a sin. At a meeting they called him a "misguided fanatic" and told him, "Freedom of speech does not give you the right to discuss freely the question of slavery, either orally or through the medium of the press."

For her own safety, Elijah sent his wife Celia Ann to her home in nearby Saint Charles. In his paper he replied to the Committee of Vigilance: "I am threatened with violence and death because I advocate the cause of the oppressed. . . . I declare it to be my fixed purpose to submit to no such dictation. *And I am prepared to abide by the consequences.*"

He soon received the message, "It is no longer safe for you to be on the streets of Saint Louis—either by day or by night."

In the spring of 1836, a series of events turned Lovejoy from a moderate to an activist.

A free Negro, Frank McIntosh, dressed up to meet his girl, was going from his steamship to hers, which had just docked. Hurrying along the wharf, he saw a man running away from two other men.

"Stop that man," they shouted at McIntosh.

Rather than stop the man, the Negro stepped aside. The man escaped.

The two pursuers, officers in plain clothes, showed McIntosh their badges. "What do you mean, nigger, not doing as we told you? What do you mean letting him pass?"

"He was a white man, and I did not know you were officers, sirs," McIntosh answered.

The policemen seized him. "You're under arrest!" One on each side, they began walking him to the city jail.

"What will happen to me, sirs?"

"Not less than ten years in the penitentiary. Maybe the rest of your life!" the officers told him.

With fear and rage Frank McIntosh suddenly began swinging his three-blade pocket knife, stabbing and killing one of his captors.

A crowd collected. "We want that nigger's life! He killed a white man!" they shouted.

They dragged him by his arms and legs to the town common. There they chained him to a large locust tree, piled railroad ties and wood shavings up to his knees and set fire to them.

"Shoot me," the victim begged as the fire licked up his body.

No one moved.

He began singing, "O, when shall I see Jesus and reign with him above?" His head dropped.

"He's dead," a spectator called.

"No, no. I feel as much as any of you. I hear you all. Shoot me! Shoot me!" he cried in agony.

Fifteen to twenty minutes later, McIntosh was dead, but the mob still had not had enough. They paid Louis, an old Negro, seventy-five cents to keep the fire burning through the night.

Around noon the next day, Elijah Lovejoy visited the scene. He found boys shooting with slingshots to see if they could break the dead man's skull.

In the *Observer*, he condemned the "savage barbarity" of the burning and the "spirit of mobism" which "in Saint Louis . . . forces a man to the stake and burns him alive!"

. The judge, ironically named Lawless, under whom the case was tried, excused the mob, reasoning that in all ages and nations "almost electric frenzy" has led multitudes to deeds of death and mutilation. He put the blame for the incident on Elijah Lovejoy and the *Observer* for inciting citizens by his attacks on slaveholders.

Already inflamed, Saint Louis citizens felt Judge Lawless's decision gave them the right to fight Lovejoy as they wished. At night they entered his office, destroying parts of the press. They broke into his home, smashing the furniture and recent wedding gifts.

When he described their losses to his wife who was still in Saint Charles, he said, "No matter what they have destroyed! At least they have not hurt you!"

Alton was a prosperous city in Illinois, a free state which sought to remain so by forbidding the entry of blacks. Many citizens believed in slavery, but did not want the issue to disrupt the state. Alton invited Lovejoy to bring his family and his paper, the *Observer*, there. It was understood he was not to dwell on controversial subjects like slavery, and he assured them that he was not an outright abolitionist.

Aside from its welcome, Alton may have appealed to him, too, because of its location on the Mississippi River, and its lakes, which reminded him of his home in Maine.

With the approval of the Presbyterian Church, largely antislavery in the North, Lovejoy decided to pack up what was left of his press and take it to Alton. The city was across the river and twenty-five miles up from Saint Louis.

The press arrived in Alton on a Sunday morning in late July, 1836. To the Reverend Elijah Lovejoy, labor on Sunday was sinful. Nor would he ask another man to work on the Sabbath. The crate was to be left on the dock until the next morning. During the night, some men, proslavery sympathizers from Missouri or

Alton, knocked the remnants of the printing press to pieces and dropped the parts into the river.

The law-abiding citizens of Alton were outraged at this violation of private property, and they raised enough money for a new press. By September Lovejoy had printed the first Alton edition of the *Observer*. In this edition Lovejoy told them that although he was not an abolitionist, he was against the institution of slavery.

In this town, in a free state, he did not feel it was necessary to denounce slaveholders as he had in the slave state of Missouri. He did not, however, modify in the slightest his stand on his right to speak out. "But, gentlemen, as long as I am an American citizen, I shall hold myself at liberty to speak, to write, and to publish whatever I please on any subject."

The minister was hopeful about Alton as a home for his family and his paper. Its circulation was increasing among antislavery supporters as well as among Presbyterians throughout the North. Abolitionists were gradually taking over most of the journal's expenses. Little by little Lovejoy began speaking out against slavery more forcefully. He attacked Christian ministers for not opposing it: "The Gospel of the Son of God requires not the good treatment of the black man as a *slave*, but as a *man*, and a moral and accountable being; the first step in this treatment is to set him free."

After Alton's traditional Fourth of July rallies in

1837, Lovejoy published this editorial: "Alas! What a bitter mockery is this. We assemble to thank God for our freedom . . . while our feet are on the necks of nearly three million of our fellow men. . . . Even that very flag of freedom that waves over our heads is formed from materials cultivated by slaves, on a soil moistened with their blood drawn from them by the whip of a republican taskmaster."

By the end of July, Lovejoy had identified completely with the abolitionists, and Alton was no longer friendly to him. He did not, however, expect the angry and vehement response that he received from the twelve men who threatened to tar and feather him and later destroyed his press. "A nigger-loving preacher who broke his word," they called him.

In abolitionist journals and in the town's other paper, Lovejoy appealed for fifteen hundred dollars to buy his third press. Within a short time there was enough money. He ordered the press, and it arrived early that fall when the Reverend Lovejoy was a guest preacher in a neighboring town. Alton's young mayor, John M. Krum, went to the dock to insure its safe conveyance to a neighboring warehouse. Despite observers' jeers—"There goes the abolitionist press!" and "Get it!"—the crate reached its destination without incident.

All was so quiet and orderly that at midnight the constable who had been appointed by the mayor to guard the press went home. After he left, a handful of masked men went boldly to the warehouse. They battered open the door, tore the press from its crate, and destroyed it. Then they threw the remnants into the river.

They destroyed the printing press, but they did not silence Lovejoy.

With his friend the Reverend Edward Beecher, brother of Harriet Beecher Stowe and president of Illinois College at Jacksonville, Lovejoy decided to call a meeting to form an Illinois antislavery society.

The day was October 26, 1837. People from all over the state gathered for the convention. Against Lovejoy's better judgment, he let Beecher soften the opposition to the meeting by inviting not only opponents of slavery but also all who wished to discuss the subject.

Like many others in a free state bordering a slave state, Usher Linder, the attorney general of the free state of Illinois, was personally in favor of slavery. As long as his attacks did not hurt his own political future, he worked openly against the freeing of slaves. Seizing this opportunity, Linder packed the convention with proslavery people.

When Mr. Beecher countered by proposing that only those favoring immediate emancipation of slaves and freedom of the press could vote, Linder declared that his men believed in the purpose of the meeting, which was the discussion of both sides of the issue. When accused of being there to disrupt the convention, the attorney general walked up to Mr. Lovejoy and shook his fist in the clergyman's face. The opponents of freeing the slaves had a majority and won the vote.

Linder's resolution—that slaves were property and the Constitution forbids taking away a man's property—passed. Linder had defeated the purpose of the convention.

Lovejoy, feeling he could now accomplish very little in Alton, offered to resign from the *Observer*. His friends rallied around and encouraged him to continue as editor. To protect a new printing press, again bought largely with abolitionist funds, two businessmen, with the mayor's permission, organized an armed militia. "You have a constitutional right to defend your property," Mayor Krum assured them and agreed to be the honorary captain.

In response, Linder called a meeting where he denied Mr. Beecher the floor on the ground Beecher was not a citizen of Madison County. Neither was Usher Linder, but no one challenged him when he proclaimed: "The city of Alton will speak for itself. It will not be dictated to by outsiders. We will not have abolition published here, stirring up the niggers of the South to revolt. . . . We are free and will not be imposed upon!"

When a motion was made to table Linder's resolution, he responded by calling Lovejoy crazy, wicked, and an instigator of violence. "Anything is better than to allow Lovejoy and his abolition press to go on as they are doing!"

Linder was setting the stage for violence. In a loud voice he told the turbulent gathering, "Elijah Lovejoy will be dead within two weeks!"

At three o'clock Tuesday morning, November 7, 1837, Lovejoy and the new militia, with Mayor Krum at its head, were at the dock. They were there to meet the boat carrying Lovejoy's fourth printing press. The men hauled it to Gilman and Godfrey's stone warehouse and hoisted it to the third floor. The only sound was the men's heavy breathing. They were startled when a trumpet note, like a signal, pierced the night quiet. Another from across the city answered it. For tense moments the guards stood by their muskets. But all was quiet.

From the third floor of the warehouse, Lovejoy watched the sun rise over the rooftops of Alton. He heard the sounds of a city coming awake as on any normal day. Jubilant, he rushed home to his wife. "Celia Ann, we have won! Thank God, the press is safely in the warehouse. We can go on. And you will feel safer."

In Alton the news spread quickly: "Lovejoy's new press has arrived!" Soon the entire city knew that it was here and where it was. The taverns began filling with rough men, drinking and boasting of what was to come. Businesses closed their doors. Lovejoy's allies were alarmed; some sent their wives and children out of town. Elijah secretly took Celia Ann to a friend's house.

When Usher Linder learned the printing press had come and the people he had aroused were ready to act, he quietly left town. As attorney general of Illinois, he would not let his presence lend approval to the destruction of property or loss of life he had himself provoked.

Winthrop Gilman, part owner of the warehouse, reported to Mayor Krum, "We are prepared to fight at the warehouse. We fear mob action."

"I doubt it, although I will say people have almost shunned me today. As if they didn't want to face me at all. But," the mayor continued, "if you have to, you will be justified in defending your property."

Early November darkness fell over the city. Around eight, a friend warned Gilman. "There'll be a mob loose tonight. Been drinking too. They're going to burn or blow up your warehouse unless you surrender the press."

"I've heard the rumors. I have given them serious thought. I will defend this property at whatever risk."

Within the warehouse Lovejoy and fourteen men, all strong antislavery supporters, prepared to fight if need be.

Nothing happened until about nine, when the Tontine, a neighboring tavern, emptied. A gang of rowdies formed a line and headed for the warehouse. Some were swinging half-empty bottles. More and more people joined them, carrying guns, clubs, and stones.

Mr. Gilman went out to speak to them. "Why are you here at this hour? I warn you that I will defend my property at the risk of my life!" he admonished them.

"Get back!" they shouted. "We don't want to hurt you or your property. But we're getting that press! And Lovejoy! At the risk of *our* lives."

A bullet just missed Gilman. Stones shattered windows in the front of the building. Men tried to batter down the door.

Inside the warehouse, one of the guards suggested, "Scare them. Shoot over their heads."

"No! Don't waste a shot," Lovejoy commanded.

Mayor Krum's appearance failed to calm the throng. "Get out of the way and go home!" voices from the crowd yelled at him. A shot went through the top of the mayor's hat.

Rioters tied two ladders together so they could reach the rooftop. A boy carrying a flaming torch climbed up to set the wooden shingles of the roof on fire.

Lovejoy came out to see what was happening. He fired at and wounded the torch bearer.

Above the shouting, the only church bell in town began tolling. Hoping that the solemn sound might restrain the fighters, the minister's wife was pulling the bell ropes. The bell rang, men cursed, and guns

156

An 1838 woodcut of the proslavery riot of November 7, 1837, in Alton, Illinois. Library of Congress

were fired. A shot from within the warehouse killed one of the rioters.

Inside the warehouse, there was disagreement.

"Surrender your printing press!" some of them argued.

"No more blood!"

"We must fight it out, if necessary to the bitter end," Lovejoy insisted. "I, for one, am willing and ready to lay down my life to fight slavery and to protect my right to print my views!"

Again Lovejoy rushed out. From behind a wood-pile two men fired at him. Five shots hit him. He stumbled back into the shelter of the warehouse and fell dead at the foot of the stairway.

He died a little more than a year after he had come

to the city of Alton in the free state of Illinois. He died two days before his thirty-fifth birthday.

To drive the mob away, a guard announced, "You've murdered Elijah Lovejoy!"

"Hurrah, the abolitionist's dead! Hurrah!" some of the rioters responded.

Marauders invaded the warehouse and ran by Elijah Lovejoy's body on their way up the stairs to the printing press. Once there, they hacked it to pieces and carried the pieces to the river. The heavy metal sank to the bottom of the waters.

Although many condemned Lovejoy's use of retaliatory force, this youthful martyr's death in defense of his right to fight slavery with the printed word stirred nationwide fervor. Thousands of people who had been silent or neutral now answered the biblical prophet Elijah's question—"How long will you halt between two opinions?"—by becoming activists in the fight against slavery in America.

This monument in Alton, Illinois, was built in memory of Elijah P. Lovejoy. The Associated Publishers, Inc.

BLACK STATESMAN

P. B. S. PINCHBACK

Governor Pinchback! Few today have ever heard of P. B. S. (Pinckney Benson Stewart) Pinchback. Yet he held more political offices in the Recontruction period than any other black man. As a citizen of Louisiana, he was a member of the Louisiana legislature, lieutenant-governor, acting governor, U.S. congressman-at-large, and U.S. senator elect. Had he been less daring and less clever, he would have been less feared and kept his Senate seat. But Pinchback, arrogant, able, determined to shape policy, was judged potentially dangerous.

A Negro politician walked a tightrope after the Civil War during those ten years of Reconstruction (1867–1877). If he gained political power, and certainly if he ventured to exercise that power, white politicians dismissed him as a threat to white supremacy. After Reconstruction, the white South lumped all Negro politicians into caricatures of dishonesty, ignorance, and revenge. Many capable, educated, honest blacks who helped lay the groundwork for future social legislation and reform, were pictured as black sheriffs, hunting and killing; as state legislators stealing what they could; as illiterates becoming pawns of white Yankee carpetbaggers.

Even worse, perhaps, white historians—and practically all have been white—have ignored able black statesmen and consigned them to oblivion. Pinchback was one of these statesmen.

He was the son of a white planter, Major William Pinchback, from Holmes County, Mississippi, and of a slave-mother, Eliza Stewart. His father took Eliza to Philadelphia, where they lived for some years; and he was so fond of her that, in 1836, he set her free. Two of their sons, Pinckney and Napoleon, handsome and bright boys, were sent to a private academy in Cincinnati, which catered to children of unions like that of their parents.

Not long before Major Pinchback's death, he and his black mistress and all their children returned to Mississippi. As long as he lived, there was no problem about Eliza's freedom. After the Major's death, however, his relatives threatened to enslave the mother and her children. The black family fled to Cincinnati, and nothing more is known of them. With the exception of one.

Young Pinckney by the age of twelve was a cabin

boy on canal boats running between Cincinnati and Toledo. By fourteen, he had moved on to the big boats of the Mississippi and Missouri rivers.

In his eight years as cabin boy, young Pinch, as he was called, learned more than the duties of cabin boy. His "teacher," George H. Devol, author of *Forty Years a Gambler on the Mississippi,* boasts that Pinch was "his boy." Devol said, "I raised him and trained him. I took him out of a steamboat barbershop. I instructed him in the mysteries of cardplaying and he was an apt pupil."

One night when the *Doubloon* was leaving New Orleans, a team of cardsharps was on board—Pinch among them.

Devol staked Pinch. "You go down to the Negro deck. Open a game of shuck duck with the passengers there. We'll open in the cabin."

Luck ran with them that evening. There was hardly a man on board who didn't play a game and "lose his bundle."

Under the protection of fog rolling in over the river, Pinch packed the winnings in valises. He and Devol left the boat about thirty miles from New Orleans and walked to Kennersville to catch a train back to the city. The fog turned to drizzle. About every ten steps the men slipped and slithered in the mud.

Pinch, groaning under his load of valises, spoke up in riverboat talk, "Tell you what it is, Master Devol.

161

P. B. S. *Pinchback as a young man.*
The Schomburg Collection, New
York City

I'll be dumbed if this ain't rough on Pinch. I'm going
to do better than this toting old faro tools."

"What's that, Pinch? What you going to do?"

"I'm going to get into that old legislature, and I'll
make Rome howl if I get there."

Pinchback was soon living in New Orleans. His
friends were descendants of free Haitians who had
come to Louisiana when it was a U.S. territory. Many
were wealthy, and some had been educated abroad.
They called themselves white or black depending
upon their own choice or upon the tint of their skin.
Pinchback himself, who looked more Spanish or
Italian than Negro, chose to identify with those
declaring themselves Negro.

After his marriage to a beautiful mulatto, he
continued his work on the river and rose to the rank
of steward, the highest rank a Negro could achieve on
the boats. He was on the *Alonzo Childs* when, early
in the Civil War (1862), it ran up the Yazoo River to
escape the Yankee fleet. Abandoning the boat and his
river life forever, he made it through the Confederate
lines to New Orleans. There, becoming involved in a

162

street brawl, he was sent to the workhouse for two years on the charge of stabbing a man with the intent to kill.

Within three months of his imprisonment, however, Union officers granted him release on condition that he recruit a Negro regiment in New Orleans.

At the same corner where he had stabbed a man, Pinchback set up his recruiting office. Inside thirty days he had a company ready for muster. In spite of verbal promises of a commission, he was denied the captaincy of the company because of his color.

When the new commander, General Banks, took charge, Pinchback again hoped for army recognition. Had not General Banks authorized him to recruit the company of Negro cavalry? But after the men were sworn in, the general refused to commission him.

Thoroughly disgusted with this discrimination, Pinchback swore he was through with the Union army.

But he could not forget his desire to have a commission in the Union Army. If he could not have fair play in Louisiana because of his color, surely Mr. Lincoln in Washington was a man dedicated to equality. Pinchback went to Washington to entreat the Republican president to permit him to raise a company of Negro men in Indiana and Ohio. He reached Washington only to learn of the surrender of the Confederacy.

With the congressional passage of the Reconstruction Acts, Pinchback saw new fields opening to him. Rushing back to New Orleans, he played his first card in the political game. In April of 1867, he organized the Fourth Ward Republican Club. During the following six months, he became increasingly active in the Republican Party of Louisiana, which was composed of white carpetbaggers from the North and Negroes just out of slavery and some long free. The party elected him a delegate to the state convention to establish a state constitution and a civil government loyal to the Union.

A leader at the convention, he stood for universal suffrage and the ballot for Confederates. He nominated Oscar J. Dunn, an ex-slave of ability and character, for lieutenant-governor. Under the state constitution he had helped write, Pinchback was elected state senator and so fulfilled his early prophecy of entering the legislature.

At the same time, he was successful in other fields. With C. C. Antoine he opened a business in buying and selling commodities, chiefly cotton, on commission. More important, he secured the controlling interest in a New Orleans paper, *The Weekly Louisianian.* On its masthead it carried the slogan, "Republican at All Times and Under All Circumstances."

Five weeks later the paper announced: "We commence today the publication of the Journal of the House of Representatives, voted to us on Thursday last by that Body." This gave Pinchback further power and helped make him undisputed political boss of the state.

A paper owned by Pinchback could not be silent on current Negro problems. Since he was to be president of the Republican State Convention in August, he sent his wife and four children without him to Saratoga, New York, for their usual summer vacation. Although Mrs. Pinchback was ill, she and her children were not allowed to use the berths they had purchased. The incident sparked articles in *The Louisianian* on Jim Crow laws. Other subjects prominent in the paper are not unlike those we read about in papers today: integrated schools, civil rights, Negro suffrage, the Ku Klux Klan.

Later that same year, lieutenant-governor Oscar J. Dunn died. This gave Pinchback the opportunity to run for the office on a pro-tem basis and if he won he would automatically become president of the State Senate. After a whirlwind campaign, Pinchback won by the narrow margin of two votes. Six Negroes in the Senate were among those who had voted against him.

Much as his friends rejoiced at his victory, his enemies were enraged. A power struggle between two factions in the Republican Party followed. Pinchback was the symbol of the radical group known as the Custom House Faction. It was committed to freedom, to full civil rights, and to harsh terms for readmitting rebel states to the Union.

165

Governor Warmoth headed the rival faction called White Republicans. He sought support from the Democrats, who were not citizens in good standing, since they had so recently been against the Union and for the Confederacy. Warmoth, himself a former Union officer, had come to Louisiana in 1865 with the carpetbaggers. Now, however, he was not hesitating to appoint former Confederates to office. To broaden his support in the state and stay in office, he presided over a government of corruption and low political morality.

Determined to promote decency and justice in Louisiana and to hold strong against Warmoth, Pinchback, as lieutenant-governor, was ready to play high stakes.

In September of 1872, Lieutenant-Governor Pinchback, after campaigning in Maine for Congressman James B. Blaine, went to the national Republican headquarters in New York City.

"What are our chances of carrying Louisiana?" the Republican Chairman, William E. Chandler, asked him.

"Not a chance!" Pinchback explained the voter registration and election laws which in Warmoth's hands allowed fraud and oppression. "It's so bad that all groups insisted on new election laws. They passed them in the final five days of the last legislative session."

"What's the difficulty then?"

"Governor Warmoth has to sign them before the next session of the legislature. I'll wager he won't! Too likely to strip him of power in the coming elections."

Chandler shook his head anxiously. He was worried about the close presidential race coming up between Ulysses S. Grant and Horace Greeley. Suddenly he smiled slyly and touched Pinchback's shoulder.

"Pinchback, you're lieutenant-governor of Louisiana?"

Puzzled, Pinchback nodded.

"Listen. As you know, Governor Warmoth is here in New York. In this very hotel. In the governor's absence from Louisiana, the lieutenant-governor has the power to sign a bill into law." Chandler smiled broadly. "It would be a grand thing if you would hurry home and sign that bill. Beat Warmoth back. Do you dare?"

Pinchback didn't hesitate a second. "If the success of the Republican Party's at stake, I dare do anything."

"It is at stake. We have to have Louisiana's electoral votes for the national ticket to win."

Pinchback made a quick change in his plans. He must cover his tracks and leave that evening, Saturday, as no train left New York for the South on Sunday. But he had already accepted the governor's invitation for a "bird supper" that evening. How would he explain not going without arousing suspicion?

The conspirators made their plans: leave Pinchback's trunk behind, his name plainly marked on the top, in the hotel hall where Warmoth couldn't fail to see it. Have a secretary see the governor early Sunday morning with some reasonable excuse for Pinchback's absence at dinner. Have Chandler keep Pinchback informed of the governor's whereabouts and warn him if Warmoth should leave for Louisiana.

Lieutenant-Governor Pinchback made the evening train from Jersey City.

The trip was not smooth. The next day in Pittsburgh he found that the connecting train did not run on Sunday. This delayed him six hours and made him miss connections in Cincinnati—another six-hour loss. He was twelve hours behind in his race to Louisiana! Still he had had no telegram from Chandler. All must be going according to schedule, he thought, and boarding the next train he fell fast asleep.

At Canton, Mississippi, he was roughly awakened. A trainman swinging a lantern was shaking him.

"You Lieutenant-Governor Pinchback? There's a telegram in the depot office for you. You've time enough to get it before the train leaves."

Confident the telegram was from Chandler, Pinchback rushed to the telegraph office.

"You Pinchback, lieutenant-governor of Louisiana?" the clerk asked, holding out a telegram.

"Yes, I'm Pinchback. Give it to me."

But the clerk dillydallied too long.

Now suspicious, Pinchback dashed for the door, reached it only to have it slammed in his face and locked from the outside. Tricked and trapped, he managed to squirm through the window. Too late! From the platform, he saw the train disappearing around a curve.

Some hours later, another train heading south pulled in. As he waited to board it, Pinchback saw Governor Warmoth smiling down at him tauntingly. Warmoth raised the window of his car. Pinchback ran along the platform beside the slowing train.

"Hello, old fellow. What you doing here?" Pinchback shouted.

The train pulled to a dead stop.

Young Warmoth threw off all pretense of surprise and good nature. "I'm after you! That's what I'm doing."

"Well, here I am." Pinchback replied in his best manner. "And if you've no objection, I'll go with you the balance of the journey."

Warmoth agreed. The station agent insisted, however, on Pinchback's signing a paper exempting the railroad of all responsibility: the governor's special was going at the hazardous speed of sixty miles an hour.

Later, Pinchback learned that while boarding the train in Jersey City, he had been spotted by the governor's agent. Warmoth, surmising some trickery, started after his lieutenant-governor on the first train he could catch. With the special's speed and Pinchback's delays, Warmoth overtook him.

The delays may well have played into Pinchback's hand. Orders were out to prevent—by force if necessary—the lieutenant-governor from entering the state before the governor. With Warmoth, Pinchback was safe. So in a way he did not wholly lose his gamble with the governor.

But Warmoth was not the complete winner either, for shortly after, he found himself in deep difficulty over frauds in the November ballotings, which resulted in contested seats for the state senate. He now faced possible impeachment charges.

Only half of the Louisiana Senate had been up for election. There were now a sufficient number of duly elected candidates with bona fide certificates of election to form a Republican majority. Democrats, however, without certificates of election, had met and agreed by caucus to claim enough seats in the legislature to cause an impasse. Warmoth and his supporters schemed to have the Democrats sworn in as members of the Senate without certificates of election from the state board of elections. Through this device, the governor hoped to control the Senate and to prevent impeachment procedures.

Warmoth knew that Lieutenant-Governor Pinchback, as president of the Senate, must swear in the members and that two choices were open to him. He could recognize only those with qualified certificates of election or he could abide by the wishes of the Democratic caucus.

To assure the latter Warmoth went to Pinchback in the secret of night, urging him, as president of the state senate, to go with the caucus. Enough Democrats would then be given seats and the duly elected Republicans who opposed him would be deprived of their seats, breaking the Republican majority, which favored the black citizens of Louisiana. Warmoth's position would remain secure, allowing him to veto the reform bill on election procedures and thus secure his re-election.

"Pinchback, if you do this, I'll see you are well paid. You'll never regret it," Warmoth said.

Pinchback took his time about answering. He yawned. "I'll sleep on your offer, Governor, and call you in the morning with my answer."

Once the governor had left, Pinchback moved fast. He called all duly elected senators, met them in the senate chamber, and before daylight had sworn in every senator with correct election certification. Pinchback's brave move, a daring gamble, helped perpetuate Republican control in Louisiana for four more years. It also brought about reform in election procedures in Louisiana.

Three days after the convening of the state legislature, impeachment proceedings were brought against Warmoth.

His impeachment automatically made Pinchback the acting governor of Louisiana—the first black man ever to serve as governor in the United States! He served until the term expired, a mere five weeks. Short as it was, he stands as the only Negro in the country's history ever to occupy a gubernatorial chair.

With the expiration of his term, Pinchback turned his attention to Washington.

The legislature elected Pinchback U. S. Senator. But after the election, the White League of the South and traitors within his own party double-crossed him and contested his seat.

Determined to have the Senate seat which was rightfully his, Pinchback went to Washington, where he haunted the Senate chamber during the debates about seating him.

A press reporter described him as a "bronze Mephistopheles, smiling sardonically and gliding around the chamber. A handsome man with regular features, with straight hair and curling whiskers, he glanced restlessly around, his keen black eyes missing nothing." The same reporter contrasted his attractive manners with those of the Texas and Louisiana yahoos shouting, "Nigger! Nigger!" "Mr. Pinchback is the best-dressed Southern man we have had from the South since the days when gentlemen were Democrats," he reported.

P. B. S. Pinchback—Lieutenant-Governor and Acting Governor of Louisiana and United States Senator Elect. The Associated Publishers, Inc.

His opponents, bent on silencing Pinchback as a political voice, spread slander. They dug up reports of his early imprisonment for wounding a man. They circulated a tale of his involvement in a New Year's shooting in New Orleans. They pointed to the luxury of his home as evidence of his misuse of political power to gain wealth.

Two years elapsed without settling Pinchback's right to a senatorial seat. During this period, he moved back and forth between Washington and New Orleans. Still active in Louisiana politics, he sought support by speaking to Republican clubs in different state parishes. He was thrown out of some, and fights ensued which the White League branded as anarchy. Yet he drew large audiences in cities like Cincinnati, Indianapolis, and Memphis, and cheering crowds greeted him whenever he returned to New Orleans.

Just before Christmas, at the end of two years of

fighting for his Senate seat, he left Washington, confident that when Congress reconvened in the new year, he would be seated.

Two more years of commuting and frustration, however, lay ahead of him. He spent so much time in Washington that officials poked fun at him. "Senator-elect Pinchback is in town and he's daily seen on the Senate floor, hearty as if he had not been out in the cold for three or four years."

Finally, angry and disillusioned, Pinchback renounced the Republican Party. Using pseudonyms like "Nouma" and "Pelican," he wrote letters to the Washington papers. "I say boldly and frankly as a Negro, that it is better to trust those with whom we live, even if they are stained with your blood, than to link political fortunes to a set of cold, heartless and hypocritical leaders in the North." At last he threw his support to the Democratic gubernatorial candidate in Louisiana.

Pinchback's frustrations multiplied. His long business association with C. C. Antoine dissolved in bitterness. Because of an epidemic of yellow fever, his *Louisianian* had to suspend publication for some months. He saw Negroes deprived of the vote and political power stripped from them. He saw some ex-slaves who had managed to establish themselves on farms driven into the swamps, where whites hunted and killed them like animals.

But Pinchback still believed Southern freedmen

174

could obtain a political solution to their problems. He urged them to organize. In Nashville, Tennessee, in May of 1879, he called to order the National Conference of Colored Men. Here discussion focused on questions vital to the Negro then and still unsettled at the present: the Negro and labor; the political status of the Negro; opportunities for capable, educated Negroes; race unity; civil rights; administration of the law with justice for blacks.

He also remained active in politics and gave a "masterful and effective" speech on the state debt at the State Constitutional Convention. In appreciation of his part in the convention, the black men gave him a handsome gold watch chain.

Realization of shrinking black opportunity in Louisiana, however, finally drove him to leave the state and settle in Washington, D.C. The Senate at last compensated him for its treatment by giving him Senator's pay plus allowance for mileage over the years, hardly recompense for denying such a distinguished statesman his rightful seat. While he insisted he was not seeking any appointment, he did accept the obscure position offered him—the office of internal revenue agent.

He continued to live in Washington until his death in the early 1920s. His grandson, Jean Toomer, a poet, took his body back to Louisiana for burial— back to the state where for some five weeks Pinchback had held the proud title of Governor!

175

BIBLIOGRAPHY

Adams, Russell L. *Great Negroes, Past and Present.*
Chicago: Afro-Am Publishing Company, 1969.

Albrecht, Robert C. *Theodore Parker.* New York:
Twayne Publishers, 1971.

Bontemps, Arna. *Free At Last: The Life of Frederick
Douglass.* New York: Dodd, Mead & Company,
1971.

Bontemps, Arna. *100 Years of Negro Freedom.* New
York: Dodd, Mead & Company, 1961.

Bormann, Ernest G., ed. *Forerunners of Black Power:
The Rhetoric of Abolition.* Englewood Cliffs, N. J.:
Prentice-Hall, 1971.

Carter, Hodding. *The Angry Scar: The Story of
Reconstruction, 1865–1890.* Garden City, New
York: Doubleday and Company, 1959.

Commager, Henry Steele. *Theodore Parker.* Boston:
Little, Brown and Company, 1936.

Craft, Ellen and William. *Running a Thousand
Miles for Freedom; Or, the Escape of William and
Ellen Craft from Slavery.* London: William

Tweedie, 1860. Reprint. Miami, Florida: Mnemos-yne Publishing Co., 1969. First Mnemosyne reprinting.

Dictionary of American Biography, Vols. 2, 4, 6, and 7. New York: Charles Scribner's Sons, 1934.

Drotning, Phillip T. *Black Heroes in Our Nation's History.* New York: Washington Square Press, 1970.

Du Bois, W. E. B. *Black Reconstruction.* New York: World Publishing Company, 1962.

Fishel, L. H., Jr. and B. Quarles. *Negro American: A Documentary Story.* Chicago: Scott, Foresman and Company, 1967.

Forten, Charlotte L. Introduction and notes by Ray Allen Billington. *Journal of Charlotte L. Forten: A Free Negro in the Slave Era.* New York: Dryden Press, 1953.

Frazier, Thomas R., ed. *Afro-American History: Primary Sources.* New York: Harcourt, Brace & World, 1970.

Fuller, Edmund. "Prudence of Canterbury." *American Scholar.* 18:305–10.

Gill, John. *Tide Without Turning: Elijah Lovejoy and Freedom of the Press.* Boston: Star King Press, 1958.

Griffith, Helen. *Dauntless in Mississippi: The Life of Sarah A. Dickey (1838–1904).* Northampton, Massachusetts: Metcalf Publishing Company, 1965.

International Library of Negro Life and History:
Historical Negro Biographies. Washington and
London: Publishers Company, 1969.

Katz, William L. *Eye Witness: The Negro in*
American History. New York: Pitman Publishing
Corporation, 1967.

Korngold, Ralph. *Two Friends of Man.* Boston:
Little, Brown and Company, 1950.

Lader, Lawrence. *The Bold Brahmins: New*
England's War Against Slavery (1831–1863). New
York: E.P. Dutton & Company, 1961.

Lerner, Gerda. *The Grimké Sisters from South*
Carolina: Rebels Against Slavery. New York:
Houghton Mifflin Company, 1967.

Mabee, Carleton. *Black Freedom: The Nonviolent*
Abolitionists from 1830 Through the Civil War.
London: Macmillan Ltd., 1970.

Meltzer, Milton, ed. *In Their Own Words: A History*
of the American Negro (1619–1865). New York:
Thomas Y. Crowell Company, 1964.

Merrill, Walter M. *Against Wind and Tide: A*
Biography of William Lloyd Garrison. Cambridge,
Mass.: Harvard University Press, 1963.

Nell, William C. *Colored Patriots of the American*
Revolution. New York: Arno Press and The New
York Times, 1968.

Profiles of Negro Womanhood, vol. 1 (1619–1900).
Chicago and New York: Heritage, 1964.

Quarles, Benjamin. *Black Abolitionists.* London,

Oxford and New York: Oxford University Press, 1969.

Quarles, Benjamin. *Frederick Douglass.* Washington, D.C.: Associated Publishers, 1948.

Quarles, Benjamin. *The Negro in the Making of America.* New York: The Macmillan Company, 1964.

Rushemes, Rabbi Louis. "William C. Nell." *Negro History Bulletin* 13:53–58, 71.

Rushmore, Robert. "A Canterbury Tale." *Reporter* 28:46–47.

Sherwin, Oscar. *Prophet of Liberty: The Life and Times of Wendell Phillips.* New York: Bookman Associates, 1958.

Simon, Paul. *Lovejoy: Martyr to Freedom.* Saint Louis, Missouri: Concordia Publishing House, 1964.

Stone, Chuck. *Black Political Power in America.* Indianapolis and New York: Bobbs-Merrill Company, 1965.

Tanner, Henry. *The Martyrdom of Lovejoy: An Account of the Life, Trials, and Perils of Rev. Elijah P. Lovejoy.* Reprint. New York: Sentry Press, 1971.

VanDeusen, John G. *The Black Man in White America.* Washington, D.C.: Associated Publishers, 1944.

Wilson, Edmund. "Forten, Charlotte L. and Colonel Higginson." *New Yorker* 30: 132+.

INDEX